Decide - Choose Your Own PATH

Decide - Choose Your Own PATH

Your guide to making effective, empowered decisions

DAPHNE WELLS

First published November 2019.

ISBN 978-0-473-50574-5   (Softcover)

ISBN 978-0-473-50575-2   (Epub)

ISBN 978-0-473-50576-9   (Kindle)

ISBN 978-0-473-50577-6   (PDF)

ISBN 978-0-473-50578-3   (iBook)

For interviews or ordering information: info@daphnewells.com

Cover design: The Bespoke Designer
www.thebespokedesigner.com

Editing/Proofreading: Pro Writings www.prowritings.co.nz

Tootle by Gertrude Crampton, published by Western Publishing Company, Inc.

Disclaimer: This publication is designed to provide competent and reliable information regarding the subject matter covered. However, it is sold with the understanding that the advice contained herein may not be suitable for everyone. The author

Contents

Praise for Daphne

"Daphne's book can be characterized by three words – courage, power and wisdom. Courage to take responsibility for what is happening to us and for being absolutely true and honest about our own motives. Then being able to find our inner strength and build up powerful mindset that changes the world around us, as well as ourselves, for better. And wisdom to acknowledge and sustain our "best version of ourselves". Actually, those three words can characterize its author perfectly as well! Thank you, Daphne, for sharing your courage, your power, and your wisdom with us!"

Dr Monika Barton, MBA, PCC People development enthusiast, pracademic, mentor, coach.

"I have been lucky to work with Daphne in several different capacities over the past few years, both personally and professionally. Daphne's guidance and coaching through her classes, individual sessions, speaking and writing is invaluable. She has a gift for making the overwhelming seem doable, with her kind and reassuring manner. I am confident that this book will not only inspire you but will propel you into taking action on your goals and dreams."

Gael Wood www.fengshuielevation.com

"Decisions are the wellspring of our happiness or suffering. As we enter a new decade and sit at this next juncture of humanity, I'm thrilled that Daphne has written this book. Daphne is a thought leader who I hold of the highest regard and integrity. I believe she's been critically thinking about what to do next her entire life, and I think her writing of this book and the timing of its release couldn't be more synergistic. If you're serious about empowering yourself and owning your narrative, I highly recommend Daphne's approach to decision-making."

Jay Rooke, Podcast Host www.jayrooke.com

"If strength can be defined through the magnitude of value added to others, Daphne is a talented Olympian. Dare to read this book if defining your own purposeful path is paramount, practical and relevant. Daphne's wisdom has been well-earned, is thorough, and based in the highest realm of respect."

Sharee Campbell BSc Psychology, CEO Evolva Group

This book is dedicated to YOU.

Creating your own path and making effective, empowered decisions to live a life you choose and love gives other women permission to do likewise.

You've got this!

I believe in you xx

"Flowers don't worry about how they're going to bloom. They just open up and turn toward the light and that makes them beautiful."

Jim Carrey

Foreword

Decisions are the wellspring of our happiness or suffering.

Puns about 20/20 vision aside, as we enter this new decade it's undeniable that there is change afoot, and not just new trends and evolutions, but upheaval and transformation. Political, corporate and personal infrastructures will undoubtedly crumble, reshuffle and rebuild around a new level of consciousness and awareness.

Surely any change of that magnitude can trigger fears, but I remain inspired by the fact that never before in the history of time have more people enjoyed greater autonomy and influence in our individual and collective outcomes. I'm excited about this because it means more people are able to make decisions.

We often hear people say that it's unfair to judge the decisions of those from prior eras, because we don't have the benefit of knowing the context that they lived in. While wretched decisions are still wretched decisions, I think there's some truth to that sentiment, but I think the contrary is even more so true—that if we can understand the context of era of the leader, it can sometimes make their decisions all the more impressive. And so it is with Daphne Wells.

As we sit at this next juncture of humanity, I'm thrilled that Daphne has written this book. Daphne is a thought leader who I hold of the highest regard and integrity. I believe she's been critically thinking about what to do next her entire life, and I think her writing of this book and the timing of its release couldn't be more synergistic.

Congratulations for deciding to read this book. Congratulations for committing to yourself. And lastly, congratulations to the generations ahead of you, some near, some far, who will reap the benefits of your more aligned and awoken decisions as you learn Daphne's PATH approach.

Jay Rooke, Podcast Host www.jayrooke.com

1. Choose and Decide

Ever been worried about making the right choice?

You've a decision to make and you're not sure how to go about it?

So many of us women live our whole lives for others, making choices based on the impact our decision will have on those around us.

You're ready to change all of that, yet you're not sure how.

You wish you knew how to ditch the shoulda, coulda, wouldas, and live a life you truly love.

You feel life is passing you by, and that your dream will die with you, yet your life is so full and a part of you believes that change will take time you don't have.

> *"The day came when the risk to remain tight in a bud was more painful than the risk it took to blossom."*
>
> *Anais Nin*

When the pain of continuing in the same-old ways becomes more painful than your willingness to explore new possibilities, in Decide – choose your own PATH, you'll transition into who you choose to be.

The PATH approach is a sure-fire way for you to make effective and empowered decisions.

2. Courage to Blossom

"Courage is not the towering oak that sees storms come and go; it is the fragile blossom that opens in the snow."

Alice Mackenzie Swaim

"This has always been a man's role. Why would I employ you rather than a man?" he asked me.

My 17-year old self wondered why he'd even asked me to the interview if that was his attitude. My mouth said, "If I can do the job as well as a male, why wouldn't you?"

Thankfully he did. My courage in answering his question that day, as a shy 17-year old, resulted in me quietly and effectively pioneering change in what was a male-only industry, that led to doors opening for women.

It was years later when I realized the enormity of the change I'd instigated through my courage to show up and be me.

Where have you yet to fully realize the impact you've had just by being you?

That experience taught me sooooo much and is part of why I wrote this book that you are now reading.

As a rebel at heart, I'm constantly looking for ways to bring out my uniqueness and show up differently to anyone else. To be true to me and let the real me out. To refuse to be put in a box by society's norms and expectations. Yet, as a recovering people-pleaser, there's always been a part of me that doesn't want to upset people in the process.

My 17-year old self chose not to cause any ructions in that industry. I appreciated my boss employing me and didn't want to disappoint him. That's not to say that my first few months were easy; that's a story for another day.

Several years later, when I left there to have my first child, many of the men who were particularly antsy about a woman getting a man's job were sad to lose me. They sent me flowers, cards and soft toys with lovely messages. It blew me away realizing how much those men had changed during the time I'd known them, all because my boss chose to employ me and I showed up as me.

Years later, my ex-boss told me I was the best hire he'd ever made! He worked his whole life in that industry employing staff into roles such as the one I'd done; which made that a truly huge compliment and reinforced that we are capable of anything we can imagine.

That said, it's really only been in recent years I've appreciated the depth of the impact that that had on those men, the industry and my life. The moral is: never underestimate the impact that's possible when you show up fully as you.

On reflection I realize it took great courage, consistency and strength of will to show up day after day, knowing that I had to work harder and be better at my job than any man would ever have to be, to prove a woman could do the job. Slowly and surely, I earned their respect and trust.

That experience is one of a lifetime of lessons that have come together in my PATH approach to decision making.

Time

> *"Time is money."*
>
> *Benjamin Franklin*

Time is more valuable than money. Numerous research studies undertaken over the last few years tell us that most of us believe this.

Yet, for many of us, when we're wanting to pivot or change, our first thought is 'I don't have time'. Let me encourage you by saying that the time you spend in this process will save you time in the long run.

Recently I coached a young woman, Evelyn (not her real name to preserve client confidentiality), who was not happy in her current choice of career and was anxious to make the 'right' choice about what to do next. Over the course of a couple of months we spent time preparing her future PATH so she could shine in her brilliance, so she had confidence in her decision-making and so she knew who she was. When everything came together for her, she found making the decisions she needed to was easy, which meant that the time she'd spent with me was super valuable for her, now and in the future.

Time is more important to us than money. Most of us appreciate a day off work more than the money we make by working a day, especially those of us who work for a boss.

> *"You can get more money, but you cannot get more time."*
>
> *Jim Rohn*

You need time to utilize or spend the money you create. Otherwise it just sits somewhere, and creating more can seem pointless.

In the last stages of life, people hardly ever say they wish they had more money. Typically, they wish they had more time. Time to do that which they never did. Time to spend with people. Time to give to others. Time to ... you get to fill in the blank with whatever is important to you.

Those same studies reveal that time gives us more happiness than money. It's what we want more of. Time to do what we love is what makes us happy. Time creates your memories. Time makes you wise. Time matures you. Time gives you perspective.

While we can always make more money, we can't create more time. Time has become a particularly valuable commodity in our society. Time is worth more to us than money.

As high-achieving women with full lives, we're constantly feeling pulled from pillar to post. We're perpetually wishing we had more time. Our lives feel relentlessly deficit of time. We're juggling too many hats. Invariably stressed. We've too much to do. We feel overwhelmed and exhausted. As though we've too little time to do it all.

We feel as though we never have enough time, we're over-committed and we can't seem to fit anything else in. Our tank is empty and we're giving to others from our fumes. We, women, are under pressure. Pulled in countless directions. Pushed round by outside forces. We dance amongst these experiences all day every day. No matter how much we do, as high-achieving women we feel pressured to do more. And more. It's endless.

Until you decide otherwise. While I appreciate deciding otherwise may appear to be difficult, the truth is that it doesn't have to be. At any given moment we all have the power to choose different.

'Until you decide otherwise' may appear to you as though I'm pretending it's an easy thing to do. Believe me, I know from experience that deciding differently is not an easy thing to do. The forces and pressures that got you to where you are today will be a force to reckon with as you decide.

> *"Give me six hours to chop down a tree and I will spend the first four sharpening the axe."*
>
> Abe Lincoln

Abe Lincoln knew that chopping down the tree would take time, yet he appreciated the value of the time he spent in preparation to make the job easier; then his ax would be sharper and achieving his desired outcome would take less effort and less time.

The time, effort and energy you spend familiarizing your-self with the PATH technique and applying it to your life will result in you having more time to do whatever you choose in your life.

The purpose of this book is to give you the tools you need to be more powerful, more peaceful, more productive, more profitable and more playful as you stand strong in your new decision to navigate change, start over, choose your own path, do work you love and love your life; as you courageously blossom.

Decide

> *"Once you make a decision the universe conspires to make it happen."*
>
> *Ralph Waldo Emerson*

What if making decisions didn't have to be hard?

What if you didn't second guess yourself?

What if you never doubted your decisions again?

Hint: it is possible!

Where are you resisting making decisions?

Procrastination is the enemy of decision according to Napoleon Hill. He goes on to explain in his famous book 'Think and Grow Rich' that successful people have "the habit of reaching decisions promptly and of changing those decisions slowly".

One thing I've noticed that keeps coming up over and over again, is that we women resist making decisions, especially decisions that benefit us.

We spend much of our lives making choices based on the impact our decision will have on those around us. Our children. Our parents. Our husband or significant other. And on and on; that list could go on forever.

And it doesn't serve us well. It holds us where we are. Treading water. Spinning. Unable to make the progress you want. Unable to receive the success you dream of. Unable to attract the results you seek.

Resisting making decisions keeps you stuck where you are. It's almost as though you're ankle-strapped to the spot and you can't move. Totally not desirable, right?

The truth is that not making decisions has a huge impact on you, your life and your business. When you're avoiding deciding, nothing will change. Evelyn was avoiding.

In my experience, we choose to not change because staying in our comfort zone, keeping everyone else happy, is oh-so-much-more-comfortable. It's easier. It takes less effort. It takes less of us.

It also gives us less. Less success. Less results. Less feel-good factor. Less of everything. Why would you choose that? I have absolutely no idea and maybe you don't either. You may not even realize you're doing it; truth is I didn't for many years. Here's the thing, by not making a decision to change, you are deciding to stay exactly where you are.

Decisions are how we move from where we are.

Decisions are how we get to where we want to be.

Decisions are how we take action.

Choose and decide, there is no other way.

> "There is no decision that we can make that doesn't come with some sort of balance or sacrifice."
>
> Simon Sinek

When we choose and decide, we also need to own the consequences. We take responsibility for the outcome.

Word of warning: the outcome won't always be what you wanted it to be. There have been many times in my life when the outcome has been a total surprise to me and, at the time, not always a pleasant one!

One of those very times, though, was pivotal for me in deciding to find a different way to live my life. It started me searching for my PATH to choose my own future and use my courage to blossom.

I was a chaotic mess. My life was spiraling out of control. Constantly on the go. Doing, doing, doing and then some more doing. Feeling frazzled and frantic. Working my part-time job as well as building my business, whilst a solo-parent of four.

Looking back, it should have come as no surprise when I hit the wall and the bus got me, at the same time.

I crashed and burned. I burned out. AGAIN. For the umpteenth time! I'd been giving all the time. Bits of me. To other people. To my kids. To my clients. To everyone who wanted a piece of me if the truth's known. I was all used up. My tank was empty. My well was dry.

I was juggling too many hats. I was stressed and overwhelmed. I had way too much to do. I felt exhausted all the time. And then all of a sudden, I stopped, and couldn't do anything for anyone. I couldn't eat, I couldn't sleep, I couldn't do anything; that's when I began to feel an overwhelming sense of guilt and failure that I couldn't just keep on going.

I remember feeling as though just keeping going and giving to everyone all the time was what my life was about, as though it was what was expected of me. I didn't know any different. I didn't know what I didn't know. I'd not been caring for myself. Neither had anyone else. I'd been giving all the time.

That way of living was clearly no longer an option for me, yet it was all I knew. I'm not blaming anyone here, because the truth is it's my responsibility to care for myself. Period. And I wasn't. At all. This all happened a good few years ago now. I lived in a small community and I truly was alone!

I remember feeling like a complete and absolute failure. My business had been supporting me and my kids. I absolutely loved the work I was doing. My clients loved the results they received from working with me.

Yet, because this thing I loved was sucking the life out of me and leaving me a burned-out wreck, I was too scared to keep going. My fear was too great; my sense of aloneness was overwhelming.

On the outside, I looked successful and my business looked successful. On the inside, I sure didn't feel successful. I literally walked away from my business. Honestly, that's what I did. I couldn't see that I had any other choice. I had neither the energy nor the support I knew I needed to rebuild it. I knew enough to know that I couldn't rebuild it in the same way I'd built it originally.

> "We cannot solve our problems by using the same kind of thinking we used when we created them."

> Albert Einstein

The reality is that I'm not the only one who's ever felt that way. Many of us feel like walking away from time to time. When I walked away from my business, I truly felt it was my only option. I couldn't find anyone to help me and I just didn't know what else to do. It certainly wasn't an easy decision to make.

The grief and regret I felt after walking away was overwhelming. For many months afterwards, I received calls and visits from women eagerly seeking my services. Turning them away was heart-wrenching. I'd have given anything to have received help and support so that I could stay in my business. Sadly, nothing was available at that time.

A huge part of why I do what I do is so that I can serve and support women, so you don't have to do it all alone and so you don't sacrifice yourself in the process, as I did.

That experience led me to discover the PATH approach to demystifying decisions, navigating change, starting over and creating a life you love.

Decisions are way more important than most people think.

The decisions we make affect everything in our world.

How we make decisions affects everything. Our results. Our success. Our business. Our life. Our relationships. Our everything.

My life. Your life. Every human's life. Every business's life. Is a series of decisions.

> "Don't find fault, find a remedy."
>
> Henry Ford

This wisdom from Henry Ford relates closely to what we're talking about here. While you could go down a rabbit hole to find out why you're where you are, I encourage you to proactively find and become the remedy to your situation.

> *"Life is a series of decisions and reactions … And then it's over."*
>
> Noah Hawley

Each decision you make affects your life.

> *"It is in your moments of decision that your destiny is shaped."*
>
> Tony Robbins

Decisions you choose not to make also affect you.

How, then, can we ensure we're making effective, empowering decisions?

Empowering decisions are decisions that create change. Decisions that make a difference.

Empowering decisions shape your destiny. Decisions that change someone's life for good.

> *"The quality of decision is like the well-timed swoop of a falcon which enables it to strike and destroy its victim."*
>
> Sun Tzu

The falcon lines up his prey. The falcon times his swoop so he will strike his prey at the best possible time. The falcon decides and swoops. The quality of his decision is measured by whether he successfully strikes and destroys his victim.

That's a lot going on there for the falcon!

Many of us humans have a history of making decisions that seem like we're jumping all over the place. Going from one hot potato to another. From one bright, shiny object to another.

It appears as though we're in action, making progress, creating momentum and moving right along. Reality, however, can paint a very different picture.

When we're busily zapping from one thing to another, the reality is that we can be just treading water. Staying stuck in the same spot. Creating waves, sure. Making noise to be sure. Creating results and change? Not so much.

Almost as though we're being Tootle*[1]; playing in the meadow, dancing in the buttercups, watching frogs and making daisy chains rather than practicing staying on the rails no matter what.

1. *Being a mum of four children, I loved reading stories to them all, each and every day. As well as using gardening analogies, I frequently use stories when working with my clients to communicate concepts more clearly. "Tootle", by Gertrude Crampton, is one I'll use throughout this book as it applies beautifully to my PATH process.

The truth is that when you discover and use your own PATH to making decisions, you truly can be more powerful, more peaceful, more productive, more profitable and more playful.

It's important to me that you know this is not a book full of answers. This is an interactive piece of work. You'll be given questions to answer and reflect on. And, of course, there's actions for you to undertake so that you can create your own unique PATH.

Packed into this book is material I've only previously shared with my private clients, masterminds and group program participants. Through reading this book and implementing the actions suggested, as well as those you identify while reflecting on the contents, you'll receive huge value.

A word of warning here, doing this on your own is going to be hard. Harder than it needs to be.

When you join my VIPs, you'll receive gifts, big discounts, promotions and special private event invites. To be a VIP and receive all the bonuses available with this book pop on over to https://daphnewells.com/decidebookdownloads/

Let's explore the PATH way ...

And create YOUR PATH ...

Your unique PATH to empowering decisions.

To removing the mystery from making decisions.

Your unique PATH to making clear decisions.

Your unique PATH to navigating change.

Your unique PATH to starting over.

Your unique PATH to using your courage to blossom.

Empowering you to do work you love and love your life.

PATH – say, what?

> *"If you want to succeed you should strike out on new paths, rather than travel the worn paths of accepted success."*
>
> *John D Rockefeller*

My journey led me to discovering the PATH way to make empowered decisions.

Paths vary tremendously from one to another. Just as we humans do.

Paths vary from region to region, from culture to culture, from home to home.

The path you choose in your life will be unique to you. This approach is not a cookie-cutter, paint-by-numbers system. You'll create the PATH that will work for you.

The PATH way consists of four pillars. These pillars are: prepare, active, trust and hero. You'll choose your own path using these pillars.

Prepare is where you experience the power of preparing your foundations and choosing consciously. This pillar consists of three parts; making courageous choices, building firm foundations and creating beneficial boundaries.

Active increases your awareness of the impact that consistent, constructive action has on you, your life and everything around you. Here, you explore your future focus, your stick-to-it-ivness and prioritizing for progress.

Trust allows you to enhance your willingness to trust yourself through owning your truth, managing your mindset and expanding your sustainability.

Hero encourages you to accept and love the hero inside of you. Yes, we all are one! Here, you explore yourself as a champion, the selflessness of self-care and the necessity for us all to be part of a community of connection.

The more comfortable you become with this process, the more comfortable you'll be with creating your own individually unique path to navigate change, so you have more time to do what you love.

Be assured that this method works. I've used it with my clients in private coaching, masterminds and group programs. It works when you personalize it to your uniqueness, and take the required actions.

Let's get started on your PATH!

3. Pillar 1: Prepare

"Confidence is preparation in action."

Ron Howard

Constructing any path starts with preparation.

Pretend for a moment that you're creating a concrete pathway.

Imagine that you choose not to do any preparation; you pour the concrete over the lawn where you want the path to go.

How long will you expect it to last before it cracks?

How much time will pass before the concrete breaks or the grass pokes through in the thinner places?

Will your path take on the shape you intend it to?

How far will the concrete spread?

If you want your path to stand the test of time, preparation is essential to ensure you have a firm foundation on which to lay the concrete, so it won't crack and break up. That way, your path is a more stable structure and will be useful to you for longer.

Initially, you'll need to choose your destination. Where will your path lead?

In order for your path to reach your chosen destination,

you'll need to determine its shape and size. You'll need to create borders and boundaries to contain your path.

Remember the falcon? He knew what he had to take into consideration in choosing when to swoop on his prey. He prepared by taking a bird's eye view of his prey and determining his moment of decision.

Our friend Tootle was attending the Lower Trainswitch School for Trains, preparing himself to be a Flyer. Attending lessons in Whistle Blowing, Puffing Loudly When Starting, Stopping for a Red Flag Waving, Pulling the Diner without Spilling the Soup and Staying on the Rails No Matter What.

Both the falcon and Tootle prepared themselves for the choices and decisions they made.

It's essential to prepare the ground below where you want to create a path so that it will maintain its structure and stability.

Choices are the beginning of your preparation.

If it's important for the falcon and Tootle to spend time in preparation ... then it stands to reason it's all the more so for us as humans.

As women, mothers, daughters, grannies, friends, wives, partners, leaders, business owners, entrepreneurs, aunties, and ... fill in the blank ... preparation is vitally important.

Let's prepare ...

We prepare by choosing courageously.

We follow that by creating firm foundations.

We then build beneficial boundaries.

Let's begin …

4. Step 1: Courageous Choices

"I am very proud of my mom and consider her the most courageous woman I know. With perseverance, sacrifice and hard work, she raised a family and gave us the tools and spirit to succeed. That is something I will always be thankful for."

Diana Lopez

Some time ago I was coaching a woman, Wanda (not her real name). We'd been working together for several months and during that time she'd worked through a lot; a big lot of stuff. She'd made heaps of changes in her life and we both felt she was making really great progress.

I did, however, have this nagging feeling there was a big road block in her way, stopping her from making fabulous headway. I'd glimpsed it. She'd allowed me to peek at it briefly. Then she'd shut the door, refusing to look more closely.

For weeks; months really, she skirted round this issue, refusing to acknowledge it even existed. Then, one magical day, she picked it up and played with it.

"Ooooh, now I get it" she said exuberantly. She opened the door and we dug deeper. Finally, she felt ready. And she dove in, boots and all. The next time we spoke, she literally blew me away with the leaps and strides she had made in her life.

Effectively, she had changed just about everything in her life to become what she had dreamed it would be when we initially started working together. She'd moved towns, changed jobs, moved away from living with family. She was no longer at the beck and call of her family. She'd stopped jumping to their demands, dancing to their tune. She was making decisions based on what she wanted. Wanda had made courageous choices.

My heart jumped for joy. For her. For her family. For everyone in her life.

Mostly for her. What Wanda had courageously acknowledged was that she was living her life as prescribed by her mother, by her brother, by her family, by her cultural norms and expectations. In the process, the ripples she made also benefited her family.

Choice is Key

> *"Today is the day of decision."*
>
> Joseph B Wirthlin

Choose then decide ... there is no other way!

Your life is a procession of decisions.

> *"Our life is the sum total of all the decisions we make every day."*
>
> Myles Munroe

Your journey through life is a series of decisions. Each decision you make leads to a result. Then you make another decision. Usually each decision is based on how we feel about the results our last decision achieved.

After each decision you take action. Action is part of attraction. Without action, there is no attraction. No movement. No results.

First, before anything else, comes a choice.

Then a decision to make the choice.

Then action to implement the decision.

You choose your life. You choose. It's your decision.

> "Be miserable. Or motivate yourself. Whatever has to be done, it's always your choice."
>
> Wayne Dyer

Who will you be? What will your life be?

Will you stay as you are? Will you choose to change so you can achieve whatever you desire?

You get to choose.

> "There's a lot of randomness in the decisions that people make."
>
> Daniel Kahneman

Truth is, you get to choose whether your decisions are random or not! Choice is key.

Your choices impact you.

Choices are everywhere.

Which will you choose? What will you choose?

Your life is a succession of choices.

We make a choice and then another confronts us. And another. And another. And we rinse and repeat all day. We're constantly making choices. Every minute. Every hour. Every day. Every week. Every month. Every year.

The problem is that most of us are unaware of how many choices we actually make. As a recovering people-pleaser, my past is littered with a long line of choices I made to please others.

We're unaware of WHAT choices we actually make! When we're not aware, we make choices by default. We choose what has become automatic for us. When we do that, we rinse and repeat what we always do. We become creatures of habit. Living an automated life. Going through the motions of living.

Choices really are everywhere! When you arrive at a fork in the road, which direction will you choose?

The road less traveled that will get you to your desired destination? Or the road you habitually travel? Which will you choose?

As with everything in life, awareness is key. When you notice and are aware that you're making a choice, or that you have a choice to make, then and only then can you choose consciously and courageously.

Leading lady or best friend?

Which are you currently choosing?

Are you the leading lady in your life? Is that the role you play? Or are you the best friend?

I remember waking one morning and my first thoughts were, "What am I doing? Where am I? Whose life am I living?"

Those questions came into my mind many times during that day. Slowly, I came to realize that I wasn't living my own life; I was living someone else's dream life. I wasn't being true to myself, rather I was being the woman others wanted me to be. Over the course of the next few days, the fullness of the web I was entrapped in became apparent to me.

With that realization, I wondered why I'd not woken up earlier. It hit me like a ton of bricks that this was the reason I felt distant from my children, my family and my friends.

My choices had certainly impacted me. Big time. I wasn't living my own life. I wasn't choosing consciously or courageously. I was choosing by default. I definitely wasn't playing the leading lady role in my own life.

When you're allowing other people to control you, as I was; when you're being a people pleaser, as I was, you're playing the best friend role in your own life!!! When I realized that, everything changed!

What about you? Are you playing the leading role in your own life?

Play with me here please ...

Which life are you living?

Are you Mrs A or Mrs B?

Mrs A: *"Oh, really, how am I going to get this all done? I have to get these quotes emailed today. I can't believe it's time already to go collect the kids from school, take Jane to swimming and Bobby to rugby. I've got to come back here and get these orders ready to go out. Then I'll have to pick up the kids again. Home to cook dinner, help kids with homework, get them settled and off to bed. Then there's wages for me to process and pay, and bills to pay …"*

Mrs B: *"I feel so excited looking at all these enquiries for quotes for this, that and the other. Not to mention all the positive responses I'm receiving from previous quotes. I'm so relieved that Steph packs all the orders ready to go for me. I've got time to do the wages, pay these invoices before I collect Jane and Bobby from school. Then I'll relax and watch them at swimming and rugby and help them with homework while dinner cooks. I wonder what's going to happen in my novel tonight?"*

Which of these two scenarios is closer to your current reality? Be honest here. This is between you and you, remember. You're only cheating yourself if you don't tell yourself the truth about this.

When I read these scenarios aloud to a room full of women, I notice that the body reactions as the women listen is vastly different from one scenario to another. I'm guessing you also experienced some of that as you read them. The truth is that many of us live our entire lives as Mrs A, up till we choose differently.

What that means is that we live our lives reactively, being

pushed round by outside influences. Effectively, it means we're not in control of our own life.

When we do that, we're not playing the leading lady in our own life!

Remember "The Holiday" movie?

Arthur Abbott: *"Iris, in the movies we have leading ladies and we have the best friend. You, I can tell, are a leading lady, but for some reason, you're behaving like the best friend."*

Iris: *"You're so right. You're supposed to be the leading lady of your own life, for God's sake…"*

What would Arthur Abbott say to you?

If he said the same to you as he did to Iris, how would you respond? Would you agree as readily as Iris did?

What changes would you make as a result?

Playing the leading lady role in your own life compels you to take proactive action.

Playing the lead role in your life requires you to make courageous, conscious choices. In contrast, really living means being aware of each choice we make.

If we truly seek to live a life we choose, then it's vital we become proactive in our choices.

That we become conscious about our choices.

> *"You write your life story by the choices you make."*
>
> *Helen Mirren*

Choosing consciously. Choosing wisely. Choosing courageously.

Choosing who you want to be in each moment.

Fully aware of the consequences of each choice you make.

Fully aware that you are making a choice.

Will it move you closer to fulfilling your goals? Your dreams? Your vision? Your passion? Your purpose?

Or will your choice take you where you've always gone?

Will your choice help you be who you really want to be?

Or who you've always been?

Choose Consciously

> "*You are not born a winner. You are not born a loser. You are born a chooser. Be conscious when you make a choice.*"
>
> *Abhishek Kumar*

For our purposes here, we'll define conscious choice as making a purposeful decision to choose, rather than unconsciously defaulting to whatever is the easiest or most available option; often that will be whatever is habitual for us.

Making a conscious choice means you are fully aware of each choice you're making and you're willing to take responsibility for the consequences, both good and bad.

Choosing consciously means you're deciding on a course of action deliberately after consideration.

Choosing consciously takes courage, grit and determination. Choosing consciously incorporates choosing courageously.

I love gardening. When I'm working with my clients, I frequently use gardening as a way to communicate what I'm meaning, in a way that's practical, applicable and easy to imagine.

When you're gardening, you consciously choose ALL the time.

Will I harvest this fruit today? Or leave it on the tree till it's a bit riper?

Leaving it might risk birds devouring it before I get to it. What will I do?

And so, you make a choice.

Because you've gone through these different scenarios and analyzed which choice is the most appropriate one to make, whatever decision you make will be based on your conscious choice.

If, however, you leave the fruit unattended on the tree because you've not even considered harvesting it, then you've chosen by default. You've chosen by default to leave the fruit for the birds to enjoy, for insects to nibble at and for the wind to blow down. By not choosing, you've chosen to not reap any rewards from your fruit tree.

This is gardening by default. Passive gardening. Having the

tree in your property and not proactively doing anything with it or about it.

The flip side to this is that you actually can't garden unless you choose; because if you don't consciously choose to do something in your garden, chances are pretty high it'll end up a bed of weeds. That's the cost of inaction; the cost of choosing not to take action in your garden. Or the birds are going to eat all your fruit, and whatever they don't eat will fall to the ground and be spoiled.

In all aspects of our lives we have freedom to choose. What typically happens is that we don't always exercise our freedom to choose. We don't always choose consciously. We often don't choose courageously. We don't give ourselves permission to choose. Not choosing is unconsciously letting others determine our choices.

> *"If you choose not to decide, you still have made a choice."*
>
> Neil Peart

When you decide to choose, it's a conscious decision; you're then consciously choosing for you.

When you decide to choose, you've got to add your courage to the mix to create a courageous choice.

Let me share with you what I learned from writing an imaginary story in school, which will explain what I mean by choosing consciously and courageously.

Listening to my teacher review our homework, I was waiting with baited breath.

We'd been asked to write about something that happened during our weekend. Same old, nothing new, right? For some reason that I don't recall, I'd chosen to imagine an adventure, something I wished had been part of my weekend. I was so proud of what I'd written. In those days, I didn't usually put my imagination on paper, I didn't usually share it at all. Writing that story was a very brave move for me; a huge risk.

What he said crushed me to the core. I felt my face go bright red, tears welled in my eyes and I wished with every part of my being that I was anywhere but there. Had the floor opened up, I'd have jumped right on in and hoped it closed over the top of me.

All these years later, I can still recall the intensity of my feelings. I felt embarrassed. I felt humiliated.

More than that, I was fuming. I was outraged. I'd put my neck on the line; used my imagination to dream up a fun story that I'd enjoyed conjuring up and writing about. His treatment of me caused me to give up on writing. He'd told me my writing wasn't good enough, that I was unworthy and not a good person to even have written such a story.

As a result of that moment, I went through the motions in his class for the rest of the year. I did enough to pass my courses and that was all. I left school after that.

Enduring his class for the balance of that year really tested my strength. I remember counting down the weeks till school finished.

What I learned about myself through that experience is that I'm stronger than I realized. I firmly believe his comment was extremely inappropriate in front of my entire class. Nevertheless, it occurred. As a result, I chose to become more self-contained and self-sufficient. I resolved to get through the rest of the school year in survival-mode, self-protection mode, which resulted in me feeling safer.

I chose consciously and courageously to endure what was left of the year without putting my neck on the line again!

Every moment of our lives is an opportunity to choose. In that instance, my choices were based on protecting me.

> "In any moment of decision, the best thing you can do is the right thing, the next best thing is the wrong thing, and the worst thing you can do is nothing."

> Theodore Roosevelt

Where have you not chosen today, when you could have?

What courageous choices have you made today?

"How would you like to grow up to be the Flyer between New York and Chicago?" Bill asked Tootle.

"If a Flyer goes very fast, I should like to be one," Tootle answered. "I love to go fast."

"Good! Good!" said Bill. "You must study Whistle Blowing, Puffing Loudly When Starting, Stopping for a Red Flag Waving, and Pulling the Diner without Spilling the Soup. But most of all you must study Staying on the Rails No Matter What. Remember, you can't be a Flyer unless you get 100 A+ in Staying on the Rails."

Tootle promised that he would remember and that he would work very hard.

He did, too. He even worked hard at Stopping for a Red Flag Waving. Tootle did not like those lessons at all. There is nothing a locomotive hates more than stopping. But Bill said that no locomotive ever, ever kept going when he saw a red flag waving.

Tootle knew what he wanted. He was preparing himself to be a famous Flyer.

What is your basis for making choices?

Change is one of the only constants in our life. Change is around us all the time. The weather. The season. Our gardens. Plants. Trees. Children. Animals. It's your life. Time. Date. Days. Months. Years.

These, of course, are the changes that happen by default. You have no choice about them. They occur naturally without your action or intervention. In fact, you can't stop them from happening even if you wanted to. You have no control over them. Change occurs.

Here's the thing, even though there are lots of changes over which you have no input, say or control, there are lots of possible changes that you do get to choose. You get to choose whether change happens or not. You get to choose what change happens.

You get to choose how much you will change. It's your choice. You get to choose change. Or not.

You get to choose. You either allow change to occur by choosing it, or you don't. It's your choice…As Socrates says:

"The secret of change is to focus all your energy, not on fighting the old,

but on building the new."

Truth is, we grow when change happens. When we allow change. When we choose change. When we choose to allow change, we also allow growth. That also means you're responsible for your change and your growth.

It's up to you to be happy with where you are at in your life and in your business. You choose to allow happiness or you choose not to.

"Happiness is a conscious choice."

Amit Ray

The choice is yours. What will you choose?

We are surrounded by choices all day long. What will you eat for lunch? When will you enjoy your first coffee of the day? Where will you eat lunch today? Who will you spend your time with? Which route will you take to work today? Which mode of transport? Will you walk any of the way? How far? Will you partake in any fitness activities today? Which one? Will you go to the gym? Will you go for a walk? Or a run? Take a spin class? Or go for a cycle ride? What will you choose?

Yep, you are surrounded by choices all day long. Every day. Yet many of us live our lives automatically. Like we've pushed the auto switch. And handed over control. We're living in default mode. On auto-pilot.

Why? Why do we hand over control of our lives and live in default mode?

My challenge to you today is to identify which areas of your life you have given over to default mode. Then choose if you want to change that. Then decide to change. Then take action. Take control of your own life and live YOUR life YOUR way on YOUR terms.

Capacity to Ask

> *"People need to understand that it's not a sign of weakness to ask for help."*
>
> *Kate Middleton*

Truth is, when you're emotionally involved in a situation it's hard to choose the best way. Why is that true? Because when you're in the midst of something, it's hard to step back far enough to see what's really happening. That's because you're too involved. Emotionally, you're all involved in the situation.

And that's when choosing the best way for you becomes difficult. Asking for help is usually your best option.

That's where I come in. One of my true magics is my ability to help you see what you can't see. I help my clients take it and move it back so you can see it more clearly. Then you're better able to choose which will be the best way for you and everyone else involved in your situation.

Where have you asked for help recently? When I work with

my clients, I encourage them to consider where in your life and your business you currently ask for support, and where you don't.

> "*Refusing to ask for help when you need it is refusing someone the chance to be helpful.*"
>
> Rick Ocasek

An important point here is realizing your greatest evidence; your key performance indicator, of success, is your capacity to ASK.

Where have you asked for help today?

Where have you held back from asking for help?

Who could you have asked and you chose not to? Was that choice conscious? Or unconscious?

> "YOU *are the average of the FIVE people* YOU *spend the most time with.*"
>
> Jim Rohn

Jim's talking about your inner circle. Your support mafia. Your five special people who pull you forward, who encourage your growth, who stretch you, who challenge you.

Who are your support mafia?

Have you consciously chosen your FIVE?

Have you courageously asked someone you admire to be one of your FIVE?

"The day came when the risk to remain tight in a bud was more painful than the risk it took to blossom."

Anaïs Nin

Chapter Summary

- What you choose, or don't choose, impacts you.
- Make conscious, courageous choices.
- Your capacity to ASK determines your success.
- Surround yourself with supportive people.

Reflect

- What choices have you avoided today?
- Are you playing the leading lady in your life? Or the best friend?
- What is your current basis for making choices?
- Where and who have you asked for help today?
- Who are your five supportive people?

Implement

- Courageously ask someone you admire to be one of your FIVE.
- Identify which areas of your life you've given over to default mode. Choose if you want to change that.

5. Step 2: Firm Foundations

Your Core

> *"The wise man built his house upon the rock, the wise man built his house upon the rock, the wise man built his house upon the rock, and the rains came tumbling down.*
>
> *The rains came down and the floods came up, the rains came down and the floods came up, the rains came down and the floods came up, but the house on the rock stood firm.*
>
> *The foolish man built his house upon the sand, the foolish man built his house upon the sand, the foolish man built his house upon the sand, and the rains came tumbling down.*
>
> *The rains came down and the floods came up, the rains came down and the floods came up, the rains came down and the floods came up, and the house on the sand fell flat."*
>
> *Ann Omley*

Possibly – I'd even go so far as to say probably – you sang that as a child. The principle behind the words is that when you're building a house or a building of any kind, it's vital that it has a firm foundation.

Same with a stack of stones. If the stones are not balanced. The stack will topple.

If the bottom stone is not secure. The stack will not stay erect.

If the ground underneath moves. The stack will most likely fall over.

It's a universal truth. True for stacks of stones. True for buildings. True for your life. True for business. True for relationships. True for almost anything.

The great news is that you get to choose your foundation. You choose your base. You choose the bedrock you build your life and your path on.

And you get to choose whether you choose that consciously and design it so it's tailor made to fit your uniqueness. Or not.

My yard backs onto a creek. There's a four-meter drop down to the creek. When I moved into my home, it was a sloping bank with some trees. Shortly after, there was some torrential rain. A lot of it. A chunk of my bank slipped down to the bottom. The recommended way to stop it recurring was to start at the bottom and put in retaining walls, using 2.7-meter poles and placing over 1.6 meters of them in the ground.

While it was a huge undertaking that required many hours of physical toil, I know that the end result is solidly built on a firm foundation. For me, it was a situation that required a lot of preparation to ensure my yard was safe and secure.

Your foundations are your core. They're the bedrock beneath you; beneath your life. Your foundations are the center of your strength and power. They underpin everything.

You'll sink or swim depending on the strength of your foundations and whether they're appropriate for what you're building. When your foundations are firm and sure, you have a framework which will provide clarity for you to choose and decide.

Many women come to me unsure as to why their life isn't the picture of success they hoped for.

The truth is, there is a solution. That solution involves you looking at your life from the foundation up.

Your vision and values are at the very core of all you do. If you aren't clear about what you do, who you are and why you do it, then how can you possibly expect your life to be the success you dreamed of?

Own your Values

> "It's not hard to make decisions when you know what your values are."
>
> Roy E Disney

Your values are your internal beliefs. Your values guide and shape what's important to you. Even when you're not aware of them. Your values determine how you show up. Your values influence the choices you make.

Values are foundational in your life. Possibly, you've identified your values at some stage or other in your life. Maybe even more than once. What I want you to know is that identifying your values and then forgetting about them will not establish strong foundations for your life. Your values are not something you can tick off and forget about.

The value you place on your values determines the strength of your foundations. Your values are part of the bedrock at your base. The rocks the wise man builds his home on. Your values are an integral part of your life.

Your values are a guiding light for you; your lighthouse beacon in the storm. Imagine being out on the ocean in a storm without a lighthouse beacon to guide your way to shore safely!

Your values stem from your beliefs and convictions, which then guide and direct your behaviors. Values are the essence of who you are, the foundation of your unique self-expression. They help you act with integrity, and when your life priorities are aligned with your values, you are well on your way to choosing your own path.

Whatever values you have will help paint the picture of the life you want to live. What you hold up as important on the inside ends up being reflected, just like a mirror image, in the physical world around you. When you're not living in alignment with your values, a disconnect between who you are on the inside and the life you are living on the outside is created. That disconnect can easily zap your energy and derail you from achieving your goals and dreams.

In case you're unsure of your values, there's a worksheet available for you to use to identify or clarify them. You can find this among your book bonuses at https://daph-newells.com/decidebookdownloads/

Once you've identified your values, it's a great idea to turn them into statements or actions to give them more life, and meaning in your life. Otherwise they can just seem like labels that you attached to yourself. (Power-tip: This exercise is frequently a game-changer for my clients).

What do I mean by that? Let me give you an example. You may identify compassion as one of your values. You could write that as 'give compassion' or 'I give compassion to me and others'. That turns a label into a claim or an action.

How will you maintain your values as an integral and important part of your foundations?

Where will you record them so they become prominent in your life?

How will you use them as powerful tools to propel you forward?

Your values will be with you for a long time, they don't often change; although their ranking of importance to you may alter over time. Finding how to use them fully in your life will reap rich rewards.

It will take time and reflection to get your value action statements to a place where you feel totally comfortable with them. And that's OK. You'll return to them from time to time and work some more on them; tweaking and adjusting as you feel appropriate.

I encourage you to test them out. Write them in different

places. Say them out loud until you are very sure you have the wording you are most comfortable with. Display them proudly for the world to see in whatever way you choose. Remember, it's your life. You can do it your way. You get to decide. You get to choose.

The value you place on your values determines the strength of your foundations. Align everything you do to your values.

> "*I have learned that as long as I hold fast to my beliefs and values – and follow my own moral compass – then the only expectations I need to live up to are my own.*"

> *Michelle Obama*

Clarify your Vision

> "*In order to get somewhere in life, you need to have a vision. The vision brings you to the table. Without a vision, you just do what everybody else does and you are just there.*"

> *Michael Schenker*

Vision is the next building block in your foundation. Your vision is what you aspire to create in your future and provides you with clear direction and focus. The clearer your vision, the better you are able to focus and have clear direction as to where you want to go, what you want to do and who you choose to be.

Vision is crucial to establishing your direction, focus and purpose in life. Your vision determines the direction and destination of your path.

What would you do if you knew you couldn't fail? If you knew you could be, do, have any business and life you wanted … what would that be?

Your dream, your vision, is what will keep you going when the going gets tough. It's the fire inside of you that never goes out. The reward at the end of the race.

Success requires that you have a clear vision and a big why. Your vision and your big why will sustain you during challenges. They will inspire you to learn from your failures. They will keep you going when it gets tough. They will inspire you to greater and greater success.

People don't care what you do – they care why you do it. When you are crystal clear about your vision and your big why, you will become a magnet to your desires; a really attractive magnet.

Your vision statement is a broad, inspiring image of the future state you intend for your life to be. It is a description but does not specify how or when you will achieve it. It puts the dream you see and feel deep within you into words. It gives you something to hang onto and build on.

Your vision answers the important question; "What do you really want? What do you really, really want?"

It's the start of making your dream a reality. Your vision statement is ambitious and forward-thinking. It's what you desire your life and your business to become. It will be realistic and align with your values.

Creating your vision provides a very clear framework for you to use when making decisions. It's a crucial part of the foundation you build your life on; one of the vital stones in your stack.

Your vision gives everything you do purpose. It's the destination you can't wait to get to and the journey there will be truly memorable.

When making a decision you can then ask, "Does this support my vision statement?" or "Will this move me closer towards my dream life?"

What you will find is that if any major initiatives you look at making in the future don't support your vision, there is a big chance they will not be worth investing time or money in. Therefore, it provides you with very clear criteria and a great measuring stick for each decision you make.

Your vision statement will remain consistent for several years.

> "A wise (wo)man makes his(her) own decisions, an ignorant (wo)man follows the public opinion."
>
> Grantland Rice

Be willing to decide your vision; choose and decide.

Your vision will guide you through all the storms of life. It's your lighthouse beacon shining regardless of the weather. Your vision keeps you focused when the going gets tough; it's there pulling you forward.

You want a really clear picture of what your dream life looks like. There are resources to clarify your vision in your book resources here https://daphnewells.com/decidebook-downloads/

Focus on how it feels on the other side, when you've already achieved your dream business and life. See it, breathe it, believe it, feel it, and above all, enjoy it!

Check that your values are showing up in your vision so that your vision aligns with your values.

> *"I learned early on the magic of life is having a vision, having faith, and then going for it."*
>
> *Elaine Welteroth*

Next, it's time to daydream; to dream up your ideal day. I'm not referring to running off and laying on the beach all day enjoying cocktails delivered to you. I'm talking here about a regular day.

If every day could be your dream day, what would that be? My suggestion is that you spend some time living it, experiencing it, in your mind's eye, and then write it in juicy, descriptive detail.

You can either journal about your ideal dream day, spend time reflecting and visioning it, use the resource in your book downloads at https://daphnewells.com/decidebook-downloads/, or all three.

Describe it in detail that's specific, so that the Universe knows exactly what to deliver to you; and so that you know when you've received it.

You will also find high value in setting time aside to journal your ideal life, your ideal year and your ideal week.

The more details you include, the easier it is for you to live your ideal life. The more often you do this, the higher your probability of creating your ideal life.

> *"Where there is no vision, there is no hope."*
>
> *George Washington Carver*

My vision is to educate, inspire and encourage eminent leadership. My vision for my garden is for it to sustain me, so that it provides the majority of my vegetable and fruit consumption. I designed my garden with that vision in mind. Whenever I've a decision to make regarding my garden, as long as that decision aligns with my vision, it's a definite yes. Otherwise, it's a no.

You'll end up with a vision statement that will become a driving force for your life. Having a clear vision and clear description of your ideal day is also important.

A fun way to keep your vision in front of you is to create a vision board that reflects your vision for your future. You can do that digitally or physically, or both. I enjoy creating my vision boards physically as I really enjoy making things and connecting with the pictures and words I choose to incorporate in it. There is a workshop available on creating your vision board In your resource bundle at https://daphnewells.com/decidebookdownloads/

> *"The only thing worse than being blind is having sight but no vision."*
>
> *Helen Keller*

Why?

"Happiness comes from what we do. Fulfillment comes from why we do it."

Simon Sinek

Now you have your vision clear, we turn to identify your big why. Your big why is the real motivation behind what you do. It's why you get out of bed and devote so much time each day to what you do. It's why you do the work you do.

Check that your big why is aligned with your vision for both your business and your life. Tweak and adjust as necessary so it is aligned.

Your why is what will keep you going when problems arise. When the going gets tough. When you wonder why you're doing everything you do.

This is something that you don't share with other people unless you feel compelled to do so; unless sharing it is really going to move you forward. It's just for you. To hold onto. It's your reason. It's why you keep going. It's personal to you and you're allowed to get selfish here if you want to.

Check in your book downloads for resources to help identify and clarify your why: https://daphnewells.com/decidebookdownloads/

You're well on your way to learning the secrets you need to know to make decision-making easy.

Truth is, each and every one of us are on this earth to fulfill a purpose. We're all unique and so is our mission in this world. No one else can do what you are here to do. You have a contribution for the world. That's your mission. Your purpose. And your passion. Find it. Follow it. Make it your life's work.

When you find it and live it, you'll keep going way after others will stop. Why? Because it's your unique purpose. You are the only one on this planet at this time who can do it.

As Dr Clarissa Pinkola Estes says:

"Be the first, be the last, be the best, be the only."

And you will be. You already are. You will naturally be the first, the last, the best and the only one able to fulfill your purpose, to have and follow your mission, to fulfill your vision in the world.

In this chapter, you've been building firm foundations focusing on your core inner strength and the power you derive through being clear about your values, your vision and your why. You've answered lots of questions and become clearer. Regular reviewing and clarification will strengthen your foundations.

"It is not the beauty of a building you should look at; it's the construction of the foundation that will stand the test of time."

David Allan Coe

Chapter Summary

- Your foundations are the center of your strength and power.
- Live your values each and every day.
- You're more likely to achieve your vision when it's

crystal clear and juicy.
- Knowing your big why is critical to your success.
- Your why is personal to you.

Reflect

- How firm are your foundations?
- Are you living your values every day?
- How clear is your vision for your life and your business?
- What's your big why?

Implement

- Identify and clarify your values, your vision, your ideal day and your why. Use the resources here: https://daphnewells.com/decidebookdownloads/
- Display your values where you'll see them every day.
- Have fun creating a vision board to inspire you.
- Strengthen your foundations by bringing your big why into your daily awareness.

6. Step 3: Beneficial Boundaries

Boundaries are your friend!

> *"When we fail to set boundaries and hold people accountable, we feel used and mistreated."*
>
> *Brene Brown*

I'm serious here. Boundaries really are your friend. Hear me out please.

I used to think boundaries were not necessary. I put them in the same category as rules and regulations. And, being a rebel at heart, they were of no use to me. Or so I thought. Little did I know how wrong I was.

So far, you've chosen to prepare your path, make courageous choices and create your firm foundations. Suppose you go ahead and fill it now, with concrete or gravel or whatever you choose. Chances are pretty high that it's going to spread where you don't want it to go, right? And that's why boundaries are your friend.

There's huge value and numerous benefits to be gained by constructing a boundary that determines the edges of your path prior to filling it.

A few years ago, I was treading water. Going through the motions. Letting life happen to me. Caught in an intricate web of family matters and life stuff that I was allowing to overtake my life. To almost suffocate me on some occasions. I was always at everyone else's beck and call. Constantly available.

Looking back, I can see I didn't have a life of my own. I'd sold one business about a year earlier and I was now meant to be working full time in my other business.

As I reflect, I realize I was going through the motions a lot of the time. Filling in the time I spent in my office. Pretending I was working. Filling my days with fluff. Doing anything but what I told myself I was going to do.

I knew I wasn't making the progress I wanted to, but I wasn't prepared to make the changes to do anything differently.

Until, one day I remember deciding I'd had enough and I chose to take myself and my business seriously.

Don't get me wrong, things didn't change instantly when I made that decision. After all, I'd conditioned the people close to me to not take me seriously and to expect they could have all of their demands met whenever they chose.

It took time for me to build boundaries, communicate them and adhere to them. Changing habits takes time.

However, making that decision was crucial to my success, and to changing everything in my life and business.

I realize now, on reflection, that at that time I didn't have any boundaries. Or, if I did, I wasn't aware of them and certainly wasn't sticking to them.

Creating a boundary is like drawing a line in the sand. Declaring what you will and won't allow.

Boundaries create a parameter between you and the world. They're like a safety net that enhances your ability to be who you choose to be.

Creating a boundary is stating what you will say yes to, and what will be an automatic no for you.

Boundaries are guidelines, rules or limits that you create to identify reasonable, safe and permissible ways for other people to behave towards you. They enable you to pre-decide how you'll respond when someone passes those limits or refuses to recognize them.

Boundaries that you create cannot be ignored or crossed over without your permission. They are non-negotiable unless you choose to negotiate them.

Through communicating your boundaries to others, you create a safe container for you and also for those you come into contact with. By adhering to your boundaries, you create a safe, predictable space for others as they know what to expect from you. They know where you've drawn your lines in the sand that they can't cross over without your permission.

Children need to know their boundaries so they feel safe. Then they know how to behave. They know what's expected of them. We, as adults, are no different. We, too, function better with boundaries in place.

It's our responsibility to create boundaries so that we are safe and also so that others around us feel safe.

I've come to realize that boundaries are not only my friend, they are essential for my well-being.

The secret is to ensure that your boundaries align with your vision, with your values, with your mission and with your goals.

When you create aligned boundaries, boundaries become your friend as they protect you from being distracted.

Boundaries allow you to stay focused on what's really important to you. Boundaries keep you safe.

Boundaries make making decisions easier.

Wanda created boundaries for herself, and for her interactions with her family, that proved hugely beneficial for everyone. Those boundaries were key to her transforming her life.

Boundaries really can be a shortcut to getting you to where you want to go, as they define what you will and won't allow in your life.

I encourage you to rethink the concept of boundaries, and ascertain where they may be helpful in your life and work.

In the wise words of Brene Brown, creating boundaries takes courage:

> "Daring to set boundaries is about having the courage to love ourselves, even when we risk disappointing others."

What are You Tolerating?

"Because you are women, people will force their thinking on you, their boundaries on you. They will tell you how to dress, how to behave, who you can meet and where you can go. Don't live in the shadows of people's judgement. Make your own choices in the light of your own wisdom."

Amitabh Bachchan

What are you tolerating in your life?

What are you putting up with?

What are you choosing to put up with?

Rather than changing?

You're not alone in this, many women don't have adequate boundaries when they first come to me. They're running themselves ragged keeping everyone else happy, just like I used to.

Amelia (not real name), who owns several large businesses, was tolerating stuff she never intended to and avoiding change because it appeared to be the easier thing to do. Her choices ultimately benefited everyone in her life apart from her. Her health and well-being were massively affected. Prior to hiring me, she was too deep in the trenches to be able to change anything on her own.

What are you avoiding changing because staying put, leaving things as they are, seems easier?

Tough questions, I know. But they need to be asked. And answered. What are your answers?

What will you choose to stop tolerating?

Why are these questions important? Because, whatever you're choosing to tolerate is stopping you moving forward in the direction you desire to go.

And ultimately, what you tolerate stands between you, and you realizing your dreams!

Clear your Clutter

Confucius says:

> "*Life is really simple, but we insist on making it complicated.*"

How true is that? We excel at making our life complicated, right? And we wind up exhausted, burned out, overworked and stressed, with too much to do and too little time.

That's because we generally have way too much going on in our life. When we can release whatever is no longer serving us and clear the clutter from our life, we become freer to do what we truly want to do.

When you clear your clutter, you are effectively building a boundary, a safety net, around what you'll allow to influence you. You're also clearing space for better to arrive in your life.

I used to think life was all about collecting things, amassing stuff. What I've realized, however, is that stuff just fills space. As well as taking up physical space, stuff takes up space in your mind, in your time and in your energy.

I downsized my home after my children left, from a five-bedroom" multi-story home to a two-bedroom cottage by the sea. During that process, I decluttered so much stuff. Literally truck loads. Truth be told, I haven't missed any of it. Not even one scrap. I gifted some to my children, gave lots away to charities and goodwill stores. Added to that, I've decluttered heaps more since then. That process has been incredibly freeing and empowering for me as I've chosen to release stuff that no longer serves me.

The more I declutter, the less clutter I hold onto, the more I'm able to focus on what's important to me.

Pssst, if it worked for me, it'll work for you too!

> *"De-cluttering can be overwhelming, so start with that one small thing. Clean out your junk drawers. It can lead to so many more beautiful things. Start there, and you'll find yourself cleaning the whole rest of the house."*
>
> *Bobby Berk*

Clearing physical clutter is about going through your physical space, your home and your workplace, and releasing what no longer serves you. There's a multitude of ways you can do this, and I'll mention some of them here.

The KonMari Method is the simplifying process outlined by Marie Kondo in her best-selling book; *The Life-Changing Magic of Tidying up: The Japanese Art of Decluttering and Organizing.* Her method involves you going through everything in your home and office, and asking, "Does this bring me joy?" If your answer is no, that item goes.

Alternatively, you can just go through stuff making up your own process as you go. This is what I did.

I started with a drawer or a cupboard or a room, and sorted through the stuff there. I chose the criteria that felt right for me in each moment. I looked for answers to one or more of these questions depending on the item:

Does this item annoy me?

Does it still serve me?

Do I still have need of it?

Does it fit me NOW?

Will it fit with my future self?

Does it hold any bad memories for me?

Am I keeping this out of guilt or obligation?

Have I used this in the past year, 5 years or whatever time I choose?

Will one of my children appreciate this now or in the future? If I answered yes to this then I'd either gift it to them then or put it away in a box for them later.

I found I had to be tough with myself on many occasions. I'd tell myself:

I couldn't throw it out because so-and-so had given it to me – really, yes, I could and I did. Truth is, not everyone has kept every gift we've given them.

It cost me a lot of money – so what, if I'm not using it, don't like it, don't need it then why am I keeping it?

I'll use it one day. Really? Have I used it in the past year? Have I used it in the last five years?

It's better than nothing – that's just not true.

I'll keep it till I get a new/better one – that just meant I'd never get a new/better one.

I'll have nothing to wear, it might fit me one day. Truth is, you will have clothes to wear and it might not fit you one day, and even if it does you may not still like it and you may just want new clothes!

Decluttering will take time, and it will be time well spent. Start big or start small. A room or a drawer at a time. The choice is yours. Most people feel really great as they declutter. The more they declutter, the more they want to declutter.

Clearing your clutter creates energetic space for new ideas to emerge and new opportunities to open up. You'll free yourself from past ties.

Once you've sorted what you no longer choose to hold onto, remove it from your home or office. Sell it. Gift it. Trash it. The choice is entirely yours.

Clear the clutter in your kitchen by sorting through the stuff that accumulates on that shelf, that corner of the bench, or that drawer – you know the one? Clear the clutter in your office by sorting through the pile of papers that always magnetize themselves to the corner of your desk or your top drawer and put them away in their correct place; whether that be delegating them to someone else to deal with, filing them or trashing them.

Clear your clutter and keep it clear. Regular maintenance, loves.

There's also the internal clutter to sort and clear. Your thoughts and your mind. Here, you can take notice of stories you keep telling yourself that no longer serve you.

> *"My mind was always very cluttered, so I took great pains to simplify my environment, because if my environment were half as cluttered as my mind, I wouldn't be able to make it from room to room."*
>
> *Leonard Cohen*

Become aware of which friends and family members drain you. Hint: spend more time with people who energize you and less with those who drain you.

What you're doing here is clearing space for exciting, new things to come your way!

As women, we usually have way too much going on in our lives and in our businesses. In order to maintain our focus, it's essential we clear that clutter regularly.

> *"When we clear the physical clutter from our lives, we literally make way for inspiration and 'good, orderly direction' to enter."*
>
> *Julia Cameron*

Declutter your Task List

"Recently a study proved that working from a larger, less cluttered computer screen increases concentration."

Stacy Schiff

Have you ever wondered what's cluttering up your time? When you find out, then you can use that information to find more time in your day.

Take a sheet of paper and a pen and, without overthinking your answers, make a list of all the activities you do each day. Write them all down.

Begin with the big tasks that take up a lot of your time and/or a lot of your energy. Those that leave you feeling drained. In your work. At home. In your community.

Now, as you read through your list, notice whether they are tasks you love to do, or you're great at. Put a tick by those items.

Place a cross by the items that you don't enjoy, that you're not great at or that feel like they suck your energy.

What commitment are you willing to make to delegate those activities you marked with a cross?

To give them away? To hand over the responsibility for them to someone else?

Take a fresh piece of paper and write a commitment list to self:

These are the activities I love to do and/or I'm great at, and will continue to do.

These are the activities I will delegate and no longer fill my time with.

If you don't already have an awesome someone to delegate those tasks to, I invite you here to assume that you will find one. That they will appear when you're ready for them.

Beside each item on this list, write the date by which you will have handed these activities over to someone else.

Looking at your list, what's one thing that you could do immediately that would bring you satisfaction? It may not be on your list already.

We fill our time with clutter. We do stuff we don't want to do; we do tasks that are not in our zone of genius.

I invite you, if you're willing to commit to what you've written, to sign your list and date it.

You have the power to choose for you. Choosing which tasks you wish to carry out allows you to clear the clutter, prioritize your tasks and gain control over your time, rather than feeling overwhelmed and out of control. You'll be creating boundaries that you're committed to maintaining.

The reality is, making the choice is the first step in creating change and gaining control over your time.

Clutter creates uncertainty and blurs your focus and your vision, therefore, it's necessary to clear the clutter so you can focus on what's important to you.

> *"Getting things straight in your head is a major achievement because there's so much clutter out*

there. You've got to push aside the static to really hear the music."

Steve Wynn

NO!

"NO is a complete sentence."

Anne Lamott

Boundaries help you focus on what's really important for you; they keep you safe. Boundaries help you decide; they provide a shortcut to realizing your goals as they predetermine what you will allow and what you won't tolerate.

You build boundaries around what you treasure. Boundaries create a safe place for you to create your dream life and business. Boundaries provide you a safe haven where you can be, do and have everything you want.

Here's the thing ... Once you've established your boundaries, you'll then be required to hold them. To stand firm. To guard your boundaries. To protect yourself.

To say NO. And to say NO again and again.

If you fail to stand firm, your boundaries will be totally ineffective and you won't derive any of the benefits we've talked about from having boundaries.

"NO is a complete sentence."

I'm going to say that again, because it's really important. For your boundaries to be beneficial to you, you need to stand firm on them. That takes courage. It takes willpower. It requires great fortitude.

It will take courage for you to stand firm for your boundaries. Remaining committed to adhering to your boundaries, while hugely beneficial to you, can be challenging without support and accountability. That's part of how I serve and support my clients so that they can make long-term sustainable change in their lives.

Knowing your boundaries allows you to be very straightforward with what's ok and what's not ok in your world. Establishing boundaries prepares your path to creating a life doing work you love, and having time for fun.

Standing firm in your boundaries encourages you to blossom courageously.

Embracing boundaries reduces stress in your life as determining your answers and responses becomes easier.

The truth is, until you take yourself and your life SERIOUSLY, NO ONE ELSE CAN EITHER!

Boundaries are an indicator that you are taking your life seriously.

Chapter Summary

- Until you take you and your business seriously, no one else can.
- Make boundaries your friend. Embrace them. Communicate them clearly. Stand firm in them.
- Clutter blurs your boundaries.
- Boundaries are an indicator that you are committed to

you and taking your life seriously.
- NO is a complete sentence.

Reflect

- What are your true feelings about boundaries?
- What boundaries do you have currently?
- How clear are your boundaries to you?
- What boundaries can you create to better serve you?
- How can you communicate your boundaries clearly to others so that you can stand firm in them?

Implement

- Clear your clutter, both physically and mentally.
- Declutter your task list.
- Make a list of the tasks that you currently undertake that you don't like doing. That you do because at this stage you are the only person who can.
- Review your list using this question as your guide: "Which of these tasks would I love to let go of so I can be free to do more of what I love?"
- Brainstorm possible solutions that would allow you to let go of these tasks.
- Choose one solution for at least one task on your list and take action to make it a reality.
- Decide what you'll say no to.
- Select some boundaries and communicate them with those who need to know.

7. Pillar 2: Active

> *"Vision without action is merely a dream. Action without vision just passes the time. Vision with action can change the world."*
>
> *Joel A Barker*

'Action begets action.' More than likely, you'll have heard that before; it's a phrase I've heard all my life. Action creates action is what it really means.

The truth is, it's easier and smoother to remain in action rather than to stop, start, stop, start our way through life.

It's easier to stay fit than it is to get fit.

It's easier to weed and maintain the garden regularly than to do a massive tidy up once a year.

Many industrial plants remain in operation 24 hours a day, 365 days a year, for the primary reason that shutting down the plant and restarting it is a huge undertaking and it is way smarter to keep it going constantly.

> *"Action is the foundational key to all success."*
>
> *Pablo Picasso*

Staying in action requires less effort than getting started.

> *"Success seems to be connected with action. Successful people keep moving. They make mistakes, but they don't quit."*

Conrad Hilton

You've chosen to build your path.

You've created firm foundations for your path.

You've established beneficial boundaries for your path.

Action keeps you on track.

Action creates clarity.

Let's get you active!

Action creates momentum which is kept going by continuing to be active. Let me be clear here, this doesn't mean working harder or longer. When you are following your PATH, you'll find it surprisingly easy and fun to stay in momentum and still have time to have a life.

For many years, I was less active in my business during the busy calving and mating seasons when my presence was required for long days on the farm. During those months, I only had sufficient time to serve and support my existing clients.

What that meant was that I had to start over again and ramp things up after calving and mating had completed. Thankfully, that part of my life is over now; however, I do remember that the effort of starting up again after calving was infinitely harder than maintaining momentum.

Nowadays, I find the more I do, the more I want to do. Whether it's with my business, in my garden, learning or walking. The more active I am in areas I enjoy, the more active I want to be in those areas and the bonus is it never seems like work as it's all pure fun for me!

Being active can be productive or not. Usually that depends on what your priorities are and what you're focusing on. Magic happens when you are consistently and constructively active.

Being active, staying active and in momentum becomes easier when your future focus is clear.

Sticking-to-it keeps you active.

Prioritization enables your action to be progressing in your desired direction.

Let's get active ...

8. Step 4: Future Focus

"The focus is what is right before you – so give it your best. It sows the seeds of tomorrow."

Kiran Bedi

Focus keeps you moving along your path.

What you focus on is what will grow.

Seriously, it's integral in the law of attraction and nature itself.

"What you focus on, expands."

T Harv Eker

It's a well-known truth.

Keeping my mission, vision and goals top of mind allows me to focus on where I'm heading; believing that I am already there as my future self.

"I'm happiest when I have something to focus my energy on."

Scarlett Johansson

Are you? Are you happiest when you have something to focus your energy on?

I know I am. Focusing on my future has increased momentum and progress in my life powerfully and positively.

We move forward faster when we know where we're going. When our direction is clear and we have a sure future focus.

Your Mission Statement

Being clear about why you're doing what you're doing, each and every moment of every day, allows you to focus on your future vision for your life.

> *"My main focus is on my game."*

> *Tiger Woods*

Do you think he'd have done so well if he'd put his focus elsewhere?

Your personal mission starts with you; it's all about you. It's just for you, no one else.

Your mission statement speaks clearly about who you are being in relation to your vision for your life. In order to make your vision for your ideal life real, who do you need to be? How do you need to show up in each moment?

Deep inside of you, you'll sense a profound *ahhhhh* when you identify your mission statement; a true sense of coming home to who you truly are. It's the fundamental reason you do everything you do, you are who you are, and you live the life you live. Unraveling it and creating your mission statement highlighting that reason, allows you freedom to focus on your future without being distracted by other influences.

Your mission statement is short, simple and to the point. It defines your definite purpose in life and your approach to getting there. Your personal mission underpins everything you do in your life, stating why you are who you are. It aligns you with your values and vision.

Equipped with your personal mission statement, you'll use it to check and align all your decisions. For me, it's my go-to when I have a decision to make, because it's the overarching reason for my being. I know that when my decision aligns with my mission statement, it also aligns with my values, my vision and my everything.

What if we all lived our personal missions every day? Wouldn't the world be a magnificent place! I encourage my clients to engage with their mission frequently; ideally, daily. I suggest they either write it, say it, record it and listen to it; or preferably all three.

When we are focused in our lives we know where we're going. The more focused we can be on where we want to get to, the higher the probability is that we'll get there.

What could you do differently in your future as a result of creating your mission statement?

My invitation is for you to create your own mission statement if you've not done so previously. In your free resources, there's a worksheet to help you with this: find it at https://daphnewells.com/decidebookdownloads/. Once you've created it, my encouragement is for you to consider using your mission statement every day. Saying it out loud, or recording it and listening to it. There is power in repetition and in habit. Studies show that when we review our goals and visions frequently, we increase the likelihood of achieving what we aspire to.

Follow your Dream

I knew there had to be a better way …

Many years ago, when I was in my marriage, I was advised I needed a counselor, or we needed a counselor, and then everything would miraculously turn out OK. I lost count of how many I went to. I have no idea how much it cost. I only know that it didn't help. I didn't know why it didn't help.

I was so used to believing it was all my fault; because that's what I'd always been told. At the time, I accepted that. That led me into thinking I could be a counselor and find a better way, through counseling, to help women in similar situations to me.

The further I went with my studies to become a counselor, the more I realized it would never work for me. I knew enough to know that if I didn't believe it could work then there was absolutely no point in continuing studying to be a counselor. The whole counseling thing was just too negative for me. It felt too dark. It didn't offer solutions that I could work towards. It didn't offer me anything that I felt would progress me on my journey to where I wanted to go and how I wanted to live my life. You can't move forward by looking back; I knew I needed to move forward along my own path.

The sad part about giving up on studying to be a counselor was that deep down inside I knew I was born to be a leader. I knew I was born to help women and children. I knew I was born to help women create the lives they dreamed of for them and their children. I knew I was born for more. I just didn't know the how at that stage of my journey.

Thankfully, I never let go of my dream. I knew I'd find a way. A few years down the track I met up with a life coach and that meeting literally changed my life.

I realized, without a shadow of doubt, that coaching was the way forward for me to help women. So, I set about studying to be a coach. That was quite a few years ago. Now I'm an ICF credentialed, certified, professional coach living my dream helping women. And I'm loving it.

Why am I sharing this story with you? There are several lessons here that apply to more of us than just me.

Lesson #1: **Never, never, never let go of your dream.**

Never give up on your vision. If you know you're born for something then it's your duty and your responsibility to go for it.

I believe that we're never given a dream or a vision for nothing. I also believe each of us is given a dream and it's our life purpose to fulfil it.

Lesson #2: **There is a reason for everything that happens in your life.**

I believe we go through stuff and learn lessons for a reason. They've molded and shaped you into the person you are today. Those lessons are an integral part of your life purpose.

Lesson #3: **You don't need to know the how.**

It's the why that's important. Just keep taking baby steps and you'll keep making progress towards fulfilling your life purpose and your dream. I didn't know the how, especially after I'd given up my counselor training. I did still know my why, my dream, and I never let go of it.

Get Clearer

The clearer your mission statement is, the more likely you are to realize it. The more aligned your mission statement is with the very core of you, with your vision, your purpose and your passion, the easier it'll be for you to stay focused. The more emotionally involved you are with your mission statement, the more likely it is you will keep pursuing it.

You get what you ask for, right? You've heard that since childhood I'm sure. And it's true. What you ask for is what you will receive. That's also true for your future focus, for your goals, for your dreams and for your vision.

What you seek to achieve is what you will achieve, down to the detail. Therefore, it stands to reason that the more detailed you are in what you actually, really, truly desire then the more likely you are to receive exactly what you seek.

My strong recommendation here is for you to revisit your vision statement you created when establishing your firm foundations. Check that your mission statement is aligned with your vision statement. Also, check your mission statement aligns with your values. The more closely aligned they are, the clearer your path will be.

> "The focus should not be on talking. Talk is cheap. It must be on action."
>
> Howard Berman

Tootle was focused.

Tootle was focusing on working very hard preparing to be a famous Flyer. He was practicing for his lesson in Staying on the Rails No Matter What. He knew he had to get 100 A+ in Staying on the Rails if he wanted to realize his dream of becoming a Flyer between New York and Chicago.

Pareto's Law

Vilfredo Pareto was an Italian mathematician who lived more than 100 years ago. He discovered something startling that we often refer to as the 80/20 rule.

That rule basically states that small actions produce the majority of results; for example, 20% of your activity produces about 80% of your success, and that 80% of an enterprise's revenue usually comes from 20% of its customers.

Count how many items of clothing you have in your closet. Then count the items you wear frequently. You will find that you wear about 20% of your clothes 80% of the time. It's the same with the toiletries in your bathroom; you use about 20% of them 80% of the time.

Business is no different. 20% of what you do every day is producing approximately 80% of your total revenue. That also means that 80% of your daily activities produce only 20% of your total revenue.

When you learn which activities in your life are part of the 20% that are your high pleasure-producing activities, and then you perform more of these activities, your satisfaction and productivity will blossom.

As you are clearing the clutter from your task list, peruse the lists with this new insight in mind. Discovering those tasks that you love doing, that produce high yields, allows you to focus with increased clarity.

Realistically, there are only a few activities you need to do every day which are really important and produce big results. If you focus on those few things whilst also focusing on your mission statement, you'll get where you want to get, way quicker.

One Thing at a Time!

For years, we've been led to believe that multi-tasking is advantageous. Turns out, we've been wrong about that!

In some settings it is essential, as I discovered in my café and catering business. There, I was queen of multi-tasking. Employees who could easily multi-task excelled in the productivity stakes there. Truth is, hospitality is rather the exception that proves the rule.

Stanford researchers' report in Forbes tell us:

> "Multitasking reduces your efficiency and performance because your brain can only focus on one thing at a time. When you try to do two things at once, your brain lacks the capacity to perform both tasks successfully."

That's probably why texting and taking phone calls whilst driving is illegal in New Zealand.

We perceive we're achieving more when we're multi-tasking.

Bottom line is, if you truly want to be productive and efficient, you need to focus on one task at a time. Switch off everything and get it done. Focus on the 20% that delivers you 80% of your satisfaction. Focus on that which supports your vision and your mission statement. Focus on one thing at a time. Otherwise you'll keep drifting on a sea of foggy uncertainty and reduced productivity!

> *"The future belongs to those who believe in the power of their dreams."*
>
> *Eleanor Roosevelt*

Future focus is truly the way to go forward and progress along your chosen path.

Chapter Summary

- Your mission statement can be a powerful tool to pull you forward to realizing your vision.
- Hold tight to your vision, your dream, even when you can't see how you can possibly achieve it.
- Everything in your life has a reason.
- You don't need to know the how, you only need to focus on your why.
- Focus on the 20% that brings 80% of your results.
- Single focus, avoid multi-tasking.

Reflect

- What dreams, visions or passions lie dormant in you waiting for you to bring them to life?
- How clear is your future focus?
- Have you let go of the myth that glorifies multitask-

ing?
- Is your mission statement aligned with your vision and with your values?

Implement

- Create your mission statement. Use the resources here: https://daphnewells.com/decidebookdown-loads/
- Check that your mission statement aligns with your vision and your values.
- Identify your 20% that brings 80% of your results and then reorganize your life so you spend 80% of your time focusing on that 20%.
- Display your mission statement where you see it daily.

9. Step 5: Stick-to-it-ivness

"When I make a commitment I stick to it."

Maria Sharapova

I live by the beach. I love the beach. I go there absolutely every day, rain or shine, hail or snow, frost or wind. I'll be there, first thing in the morning. For me, it's the absolutely best way to start every day.

One weekend, I decided I was going to do a long walk along the coastline. The last time I'd walked this same piece of coastline it was an easy walk, mostly along smooth sand with the occasional rocky outcrop to meander over. That was before winter.

On this particular morning, just prior to sunrise, I was dropped off around 18kms from my home, intending to enjoy the same walk. My welcome to the beach was wonderful, watching the sun rise over the sea and bringing color into the dark seascape.

About 10 minutes into my walk, the smooth sand stopped. Replaced by rocks. *That's ok*, I thought, *the sea has obviously washed the sand away during the storms.* I kept going and going and going, up and down over the rocks, jumping pools and splits in the rock.

I certainly didn't anticipate what eventuated. You see, so much sand had been washed away from that particular piece of coastline that I walked for nearly two hours mostly all over rocks. At one point I even had to backtrack and find a route off the beach as the deep gulches in the rocks were impassable.

Finally, I came to a long stretch of wonderfully smooth, sparkly white sand. Ooh, the relief. And you know what, it was so much easier. The flow was smoother. My pace quickened. Finally, I could relax and enjoy my walk!

And it got me thinking how our lives can be like that. We encounter obstacle after obstacle, challenge after challenge. And we continue, as I did, expecting them not to last very long. Sometimes, they last longer than we expect. Sometimes, the challenge becomes too great. Sometimes, we give up.

Sometimes, our progress would be improved with some assistance. Often at times we continue doggedly alone rather than asking for support. Although I'd chosen to walk alone so I could enjoy the peace and solitude, there were moments, as I was choosing the safest route along the rocky outcrops jutting into the sea, I wished I had company.

As an aircraft uses most of its fuel on takeoff, so it is with many things for us as humans. The time we spend in preparation and getting things started will be well worth it in the long run when we can cruise at optimal flight altitude.

When the going gets tough, the tough get going. You will have days when staying active will take all of your courage. Courage to keep going constantly and consistently in the direction you've chosen, remaining faithful to your values, your vision and your mission. Failing sometimes. Then picking yourself up and carrying on, sticking to it.

> *"The three things that are most essential to achievement are common sense, hard work, and stick-to-it-ivness."*
>
> *Thomas Edison*

Sticking to It

For our purposes here, we'll define stick-to-it-ivness as continuing constantly in the direction you choose, remaining faithful to your values, goals, vision and mission and taking action in that direction.

> *"Don't live the same year 75 times and call it a life."*
>
> *Robin S Sharma*

I remember reading in my local newspaper at the beginning of the year, all of the people they interviewed who had set resolutions for the previous new year hadn't done what they resolved to do. 100%. That's all of them!

Even more surprising is that none of them could even remember what their new year resolutions had been. 100%. Not one of them!

Which makes you wonder whether setting goals and resolutions at the beginning of the year is a waste of time, right? It's surprisingly easy to slip into a year that's exactly the same as the previous one. And all along you've been saying you wish it could be different, right?

"If only…"

"When this happens..."

If you want it to be different, you've got to do some things differently. Period. Do you seriously want your future to be different to your past? If you do, then there is some stuff you absolutely have to do to ensure it will be.

Powerful Combo – Goals and Intentions

Would you like to be in the top 1% of achievers in the entire world?

Did you know?

80% of people never even THINK about goals – they live from day to day bobbing round like a rudderless boat.

16% of people think about goals but never write them down.

4% of people write their goals down.

1% write their goals down AND regularly REVIEW them. These people are among the highest achievers in the world.

Further to that, millionaires read their goals once a day; billionaires twice a day!

Which chunk of the population do you want to be in? Given that you're reading this book, wouldn't it make sense to put time into setting goals, writing them down and regularly reviewing them?

> *"Setting goals is the first step at turning the invisible into the visible."*
>
> *Tony Robbins*

Goals are what you want to have. You may have heard of BE, DO and HAVE. Many people live their lives in the world of HAVE, DO, BE. As an example, "When I have lost my excess weight, I'll run every day and then I'll be someone who incorporates fitness into my life."

My strong recommendation is to flip that on its head and use BE, DO, HAVE to determine your goals.

Your goals are what you want to have.

Your actions are what you do.

Who do you need to be to achieve those actions and accomplish your goals?

Let's pretend weight loss and fitness is what you want. Running a marathon is what you choose to do. Who do you need to be to run a marathon? Are you going to be someone who runs one marathon and gives up? Or are you choosing a lifestyle change? If so, then perhaps you need to be someone who views exercise as part of their everyday life. Someone who is committed to your health and fitness for the long-term. Someone who fits exercise into your schedule and runs a marathon every so often because it's fun for you. It'd be wise to be realistic about your expectations here, depending on your current level of fitness and your history of running – or not.

Who you are being is foundational to you succeeding in accomplishing your goals.

What's the gap between what you have currently and what you want to have? That gap is what you want to have once you accomplish your goals.

What do you have to do to get what you want? What are the smaller goals that are going to help you get to your bigger goals? The steps along the way to your big goals become your sub-goals.

Next, you identify the actions you need to take to reach those goals. Over the time you've allocated to reach them, what does that translate into in terms of daily or weekly action steps for you? What are the daily and weekly actions that will, one step at a time, lead you to accomplishing your goals?

When those daily actions become obvious and everything is totally aligned, doing them becomes almost easy for you. That's when doing them becomes part of your lifestyle, part of who you are. That's when you become someone who is committed to your health and fitness forever; who fits exercise into your schedule regardless of everything else that's going on in your life.

Conversely, when you set goals that aren't aligned with your values, your vision or your mission, you're less likely to stick to doing them.

> "I'm a human being. I've got opinions, I'm not always right, I'm not always on time, I don't always do things in the proper way, but my intentions are always extremely pure."
>
> Kanye West

Intentions add an extra shot of power to your stick-to-it-ivness.

Goals come from your head. Of course, you want to write

them passionately so they excite you, motivate you and inspire you to stay committed to them and take consistent action. Nevertheless, they originate from your head.

Intentions come from your soul and your heart. Your intentions are how you intend to feel after you've achieved your goals. Your intentions incorporate who you intend to be during the process and once you've accomplished your goals.

Once your goals are truly aligned with your values, vision and mission, go ahead and check your intentions are also aligned.

Put all your deadlines for completing each step of each goal into your planner. THEN DO THEM!!!

Review your goals regularly to check you're on track to meet your deadline. Remember, action leads to results.

Stick to Your Plan

> "It may take time to prove you're right, but you have to stick to it."
>
> Fred Korematsu

I've always wanted to do it my way! To live my life on my terms; to not follow the rules. Rules were made to be broken, weren't they? Or at least bent?

Doing it my way, without anyone telling me what to do, has always been really important to me. It's not always been easy. And it's certainly caused a fair amount of tension in my life, but it's so vital to my existence that I've always done whatever was needed to find a way to do it my way.

I remember, as a 13-year old, desperately wanting a pair of boots. The ones I wanted were beautiful brown leather and suede. They were all the rage at the time and it was vital that I had a pair, right?

The problem was that my mother didn't agree with me. According to her, I most definitely did not need a pair of boots and I was not getting a pair of boots. Unfortunately, that just didn't satisfy me. I wanted those boots, I needed those boots, and I was going to have those boots.

In order to buy those boots I required some money, and I didn't have any. I determined to do whatever it took to earn the money to buy them.

I was a bit of a freak amongst my peers. Knitting was easy for me and I was super quick at it. I could knit whatever I wanted in super quick time. As luck would have it, a young mum with three sons wanted matching jerseys knitted for her boys. Her problem was that she either couldn't knit or didn't have time, I really don't remember which. For me, it was a godsend. The answer to my problem; my method of earning the funds to purchase my boots.

Those boots were mine, after all, and the storekeeper was just looking after them for me till I gathered the money to bring them home.

Although I really don't remember how long it took me to knit those three jerseys, I do remember bringing my boots home. I loved those boots and wore them for many years. Those boots taught me some precious lessons.

Lesson #1: I could do anything I wanted to if I wanted it badly enough and just put my mind to it. It stretched me and opened up more possibilities than I'd previously imagined.

Lesson #2: Staying focused on my desired outcome and taking consistent action gets me there.

Lesson #3: There is always a way to do whatever I choose and to have it succeed. When you're committed to your desired outcome and everything is aligned, the how becomes apparent.

Lesson #4: To stick to my plan. Knitting three identical jerseys taught me the value of sticking to my plan and commitment to my goals.

Mum wasn't always right; I did need those boots. However, if she'd agreed to buy them for me, I would not have learned the lessons I did. Even though at the time I certainly didn't feel grateful for her refusing to buy them for me, in retrospect she did me a huge service. Thanks Mum xx

Consistency Wins

> "Success isn't *always about greatness. It's about consistency.*"

> *Dwayne Johnson*

My walk on the beach one morning got me reflecting ...

How many grains of sand are on the beach? How many of each variety of shell are washed up with each incoming tide?

The waves never stop coming. Minute after minute. Hour after hour. Day after day. Week after week. Month after month. Year after year. Yes, the waves vary in size, but never in consistency. Yes, the tides vary in height, but never in consistency. The waves just keep on rolling in to shore. As do the tides.

The consistency with which you take action directly impacts your progress. Consistency is a key ingredient in stick-to-it-ivness!

> "*I pray to be like the ocean, with soft currents, maybe waves at times. More and more, I want the consistency rather than the highs and the lows.*"
>
> Drew Barrymore

Done Beats Perfect, Hands Down!

> "*Striving for perfection is so unhealthy because there's no such thing as perfection.*"
>
> Emily Atack

Are you a prisoner to perfectionism?

Do you suffer from perfection paralysis?

I did. For a very long time. Many years in fact. I thought I had to be really, really good before anyone would want to hire me as their coach. I thought whatever I offered had to be perfect before anyone would purchase it.

Here's the thing. It didn't serve me at all well. It stopped me. It thwarted me. It stalled my progress. It delayed me. It stonewalled me.

The truth is, you can't make progress by trying to make it all perfect.

What is perfect anyway? Who knows! Really, who defines what is perfect?

There really is no such thing as perfect. Not permanently anyway.

The one thing that's always consistent in our lives is change. Therefore, what may appear perfect today, will certainly not be perfect tomorrow or next week or next month or next year.

And yet, many of us get caught in the trap of our desire for perfectionism. To put our very best out there. When, of course, whatever we offer will be just right for those it's intended to serve.

Truth is, you can't make progress toward your goals or vision by keeping yourself locked away getting ready, getting perfect. Paralyzed by your desire to be perfect.

That desire for perfection traps your progress and deems you unable to move forward.

How do you change that? By deciding to. By deciding to take action. By deciding to move forward.

Which way is forward? Forward is taking any action that points in the direction of your goal.

Even a baby step is enough. Just get it done. Because the truth is, done is better than perfect!

Keep sticking to it and taking action. NO MATTER WHAT.

Remember, Tootle had to stay on the rails NO MATTER WHAT if he wanted to be a famous Flyer!

As humans, it's essential that you SHOW UP AND TAKE ACTION, NO MATTER WHAT.

If Anne can, so can you!

> "I gave up my struggle with perfection a long time ago."
>
> Anne Hathaway

Discipline

> "Discipline is the bridge between goals and accomplishment."
>
> Jim Rohn

Discipline used to be a bad word as far as I was concerned. I remember years ago hating routines of any kind. Yep, it was one of my rebellions against anyone who had tried to place a routine in my life; teachers, parents, anyone.

As I matured, I realized some kind of routine served me well. However, it was of a minimal nature as I still perceived routines to be bad.

As far as discipline was concerned though, I still thought that was way, way worse than routine. So, logically, if I couldn't handle much routine in my life, I sure wasn't up for trying to discipline myself.

Fast forward a few years to owning my hospitality business. Routine was paramount to the smooth running of that operation. I learned that lesson very quickly and routines became my friend. So much so, that I sought to put structures in place so the routines could run regardless of which staff members were working on any particular day. Structures and routines served me well in that situation.

Fast forward again to running my businesses from home. Once again, routines were not welcomed by me. I enjoyed being free of the routines that structured and ran my life prior to selling my hospo business. My days rolled into each other. Apart from client appointments, I pretty much did whatever I felt like doing. Did that serve me well? No, no and no. It certainly did not serve me well.

My belief that routines and discipline were bad actually worked against me in building my business. I found I was spinning, treading water. Not getting to where I wanted to go.

> "We must all suffer one of two things: The pain of discipline or the pain of regret or disappointment."
>
> Jim Rohn

A huge lesson was coming for me. Once I put structures in place everything started to change.

The more disciplined I became in applying my structures to my day, the quicker my progress became.

Yes, it really is true when they say that structures give you freedom.

Structure Gives you Freedom!

Have a plan. Work your plan. One step at a time. Rinse and repeat. Over and over again.

Create a structure for your month. For your week. For each day.

It's vital that we're constantly and consistently taking action in the direction of our goals, that we have a plan and are working the plan, that we're courageously taking steps, otherwise we'll never get where we want to go.

I've found having a reminder or alarm that pops up regularly throughout my day alerts me that an hour, or whatever portion of time I choose, has passed, and allows me to stop what I'm doing and move to a different task. This prompt has allowed me to reclaim my time and means that I no longer get lost. What I mean by that is that I don't get lost in a task and spend several hours doing something that I really only had one hour available for.

The time you spend creating a structure that fits you will be returned to you over and over again.

> "I thrive on structure. I find freedom in structure."
>
> Lupita Nyong'o

Chapter Summary

- Be committed to you.
- You can do anything you want as long as you want it badly enough.
- There's always a way to do whatever you choose and to have it succeed.
- Stick to it regardless of the obstacles and challenges

that come your way.
- Action leads to results.
- Your consistency, or lack of it, shows in your results.
- Done beats perfect every time.
- Structure creates freedom.

Reflect

- How do you allow obstacles and challenges to affect your ability to stick-to-it?
- Do you seriously want your future to be different to your past?
- Which chunk of population do you wish to be in?
- Are you still allowing perfectionism to paralyze you?

Implement

- Establish your goals.
- Set your intentions.
- Create your plan.
- Work your plan courageously, one step at a time.
- Display your goals where you'll see them every day.
- Check that your goals and intentions are aligned with your vision, your values and your mission.
- Set reminders for important tasks or time frames for your day.

10. Step 6: Prioritize to Progress

"Our life is the sum total of all the decisions we make every day, and those decisions are determined by our priorities."

Myles Munroe

According to Myles, prioritizing is the way to progress. Establishing your priority, and taking action on that first, before anything else.

Arrange everything you need to get done in order of relative importance, so you can move forward toward your goals and desired outcomes; so you keep moving further along your path.

Take the B. S. out of Busy

"Being busy does not always mean real work. The object of all work is production or accomplishment

and to either of these ends there must be forethought, system, planning, intelligence, and honest purpose."

Thomas A Edison

You're busy all day, every day. But are you getting the work done? Are you doing what really matters?

What I'm hearing more and more when I speak with

women, is that they're busy; busy, busy doing, busy doing stuff or just busy.

What I'm not hearing is that their busyness is resulting in more satisfaction, more enjoyment, more time for fun or them feeling as though they're living the life they want to.

When I ask more about why they're so busy, most of them are unable to pinpoint what they're actually doing. They're not sure why they're so busy, they just are.

And that's why I'm asking you to consider, to really think about, what your busyness is achieving.

I'm encouraging you to ask yourself these questions:

Are you busy doing what really matters?

Are you busy doing what really matters to your life?

Are you busy doing what really matters to you personally?

Or ...

Are you just busy?

Being busy is almost a badge of honor in society at present!

The truth is, there is no honor in being busy for the sake of being busy.

Consider how many times, when you ask people how they are, their response is 'busy'.

Consider, also, how often busy is your response when people ask you.

"Beware the barrenness of a busy life."

Socrates

Schedule your Success

"Think in the morning. Act in the noon. Eat in the evening. Sleep in the night."

William Blake.

Now you may agree with him, or you may not. You get to choose. You may agree with part of what he says and not the rest. You may agree with all of it, or you may disagree with it all. It's up to you.

What else is up to you is how you spend your day. Because the truth is, each and every one of us has times of the day that are better than others for us to perform certain activities.

If you're a morning person, you'll more than likely want to think in the morning. If you're a night owl, you may think more effectively later in the day. Either way, you'll definitely want to think before you act, as William Blake recommends. What that means is, you'll either prefer to plan your day in the morning, or the evening before. Depending on when you think best.

Here's the thing, our lives and our business are a series of choices and decisions we make along the way. We literally create our life and our business by the choices and decisions we make.

That said, there's huge value and benefit in thinking, choosing and deciding wisely. Because your thoughts, your choices and your decisions impact directly the results you get.

> "There's a lot of randomness in the decisions that people make."
>
> Daniel Kahneman

We all have the same 24 hours in a day. We don't suffer from a lack of time because, the fact is, we all have the same number of days in the week, hours in the day, minutes in the hours.

We can't get more time. We can, however, control how we fill our time. You get to choose and decide how you utilize your time; it's up to you. It's up to each one of us to decide.

Whenever you feel as though you don't have enough time, it's either because you're out of alignment, you're disorganized or you're confused.

Now that you've identified your values, your vision, your mission and they're all aligned with each other, the next piece is for you to always check that whatever goes into your schedule is also aligned, and that it's moving you toward achieving your goals. The preparation you've done so far has given you a firm foundation for arranging your schedule to make best use of your time.

Scheduling your success ensures you'll succeed. What you schedule gets done. What you don't schedule won't happen at all.

Following William Blake's wise advice, my suggestion is that you identify when you do your most productive thinking and effective work, and then build your schedule around that framework. The more you get to know YOU, the more efficiently you'll utilize your time.

> "The key is not to prioritize what's on your schedule, but to schedule your priorities."
>
> Stephen Covey

Set aside some time in your schedule at the beginning of your day to set your intentions for that day, to review your goals, and to spend time preparing your mind for the day ahead. Some people like to meditate, others journal, others listen to inspirational music, some practice yoga or exercise.

What gets your mind and body ready to perform effectively and productively? If you're not sure what does, I invite you to play with different options till you find what lights you up the most.

The clearer your intentions for the day are, the higher the probability you'll achieve them.

> "How you prioritize your life and career is your choice. Once you make a decision, stick to it; don't always second-guess yourself."
>
> Angela Braly

I've found that scheduling blocks of time during my day and week for specific tasks allows me to focus on that particular activity at that time, without thinking about anything else. It's as though I've made an appointment with myself, and I don't have to think about it till then.

In your scheduling, remember to use Pareto's law. The most important items on your schedule come from the 20%. Ideally, they will be allotted the majority of your available time.

I recommend that you fill only 80% of your available time so that 20% can be flexible.

Proactive versus Reactive

> *"It's not enough to be busy. So are the ants. The question: What are we busy about?"*
>
> *Henry David Thoreau*

Prioritizing your time allows you to control what you do so that you're being proactive.

When you choose not to be proactive, not to schedule your success, not to prioritize what's important to you, you end up running around keeping everyone else happy. Responding to their 'urgents'; reacting to their demands.

When you proactively schedule your time and prioritize your activities, you create boundaries that defend you from other people's urgents and demands. Then when interruptions occur, you'll feel empowered to choose your response.

Being proactive means, you're initiating change rather than reacting to events or people. It means you're in the driver's seat. You're playing the leading lady role rather than the best friend. It means you're being constructively active rather than just being busy; that you're making empowered decisions and continuing on your path.

How do we prioritize? Refer to the earlier list of activities you do every day; declutter your task list. Look at the list of activities you love doing and intend to continue doing. And then number them, with number one being the top priority; the most important activity on the list. Remember to check each item against your values, your vision and your mission so that the priorities you choose are in alignment for you.

My recommendation is, you have no more than three top priorities for each day; the must-dos that will happen no matter what; if that's all you achieve that day, you'll be content. Then make another list of activities to work on as time allows.

In amongst your scheduling, when you plan blocks of intensive work that you don't wish to be interrupted from, my suggestion is that you turn off all distractions. Block your phone calls, turn off emails, turn off social media, put a sign on the door that says not to disturb. Do whatever it takes, to get the uninterrupted time you need to make the difference you are here to make.

Challenge yourself to be fully present and fully productive. Use a timer and work consistently till the timer rings. Find what works for you, and do it over and over again.

> "Nobody's life is ever all balanced. It's a conscious decision to choose your priorities every day."
>
> Elisabeth Hasselbeck

The more productively and constructively you utilize your

time, the more you'll achieve, and the more time you'll have to do whatever you choose.

If focusing intently for a period of time is not something you find easy, my suggestion is to utilize the Pomodoro technique, where you set a timer for 25 minutes and work concentratedly for that time. When the timer goes off, treat yourself to a 5-minute break. After four stretches of that sequence, take a longer break. It's a great way to power your way through and get stuff done.

> "One of the things I realized is that if you do not take control over your time and your life, other people will gobble it up. If you don't prioritize yourself, you constantly start falling lower and lower on your list."

> Michelle Obama

Eliminate, Automate or Delegate

> "If ants are such busy workers, how come they find time to go to all the picnics?"

> Marie Dressler

You've heard it before, I'm sure; 'Do what you love and you'll never work a day in your life'.

Let's presume, that like most people, you've got a whole heap of stuff you're responsible for doing every day that you love, and then there's a whole heap that you don't love.

The fact remains though that those tasks do need to be done on a regular basis, right? Same goes for the things on the list you created earlier, of tasks you no longer choose to do yourself. So, what can you do about it?

Well, let's brainstorm here. Some possible solutions are:

- Delegate the tasks to a colleague or family member
- Decide if the task is still relevant or can be eliminated
- Systematize the tasks so the chunks appear smaller and more manageable
- Engage a contractor to do the tasks
- Automate tasks that can be automated
- Plan some chunks of time to dedicate to completing these tasks
- Hire someone to handle the tasks
- Have courageous conversations to negotiate how you can remove these tasks from your area of responsibility

And the list could go on and on. The possibilities are endless.

My point here is, sometimes we get stuck in how we do things and we don't look outside of the square. We don't look at the bigger picture. We don't look at how the 'having to do these tasks' is wearing us down and affecting us in other areas of our life.

What can you do about it? Take a good look at the tasks you perform regularly in your work and at home that you don't enjoy doing; that are not part of your core area of expertise. Tasks that drain your energy; that you do just because there is no one else to do them and they have to be done.

Make a list of those tasks. Then look over the list asking the question, "Which of these tasks would I love to let go of so I can be free to do what I love?"

And then take whatever actions you can to move in that direction. By arranging all the stuff that needs to get done in order of its relative importance, you'll move forward toward your goals and vision with increased grace and ease. Laying the ground work sets you up for success.

> "My message to women is: Women: We can do it. We are capable of doing almost anything, but we must learn we cannot do it all at once, we need to prioritize."

> Michelle Bachelet

Top Three

> "Action expresses priorities."

> Mahatma Gandhi

Choose your top three priorities every day. The tasks or activities that you will do NO MATTER WHAT. The three that are priorities for you.

Check they're aligned with your values, your vision and your mission. Check they're steps on the path to achieving your goals. Plan time to complete them early in the day.

Rank the other things you would like to achieve in order of importance, so that once you've completed your top three you know what you're doing next. Having pre-decided your priorities for each day, you will flow through your workload with greater ease and joy.

"The most difficult thing is the decision to act, the rest is merely tenacity. The fears are paper tigers. You can do anything you decide to do. You can act to change and control your life; and the procedure, the process is its own reward."

Amelia Earhart

Chapter Summary

- Ditch the B. S. and do what really matters.
- Prioritize ruthlessly.
- Be proactive rather than reactive.
- Remember to check your priorities are aligned.

Reflect

- Where are you idealizing busy?
- Which end of the day is best for you to plan and schedule your day?
- What are your top priorities and how are they reflected in your daily activities?
- What can you eliminate, automate or delegate?

Implement

- Schedule your top 3 every day.
- Schedule time blocks for specific activities.
- Trial the Pomodoro technique to assess whether it's a useful tool for you.
- How can you effectively eliminate, automate or delegate those tasks that you no longer choose to do yourself?

11. Pillar 3: Trust

"Trust is built with consistency."

Lincoln Chafee

Trust is vital. To you. To your life. To your very existence.

"Trust yourself. Create the kind of self that you will be happy to live with all your life. Make the most of yourself by fanning the tiny, inner sparks of possibility into flames of achievement."

Golda Meir

Trust at its core begins with you trusting you, trusting your truth; you listening to your inner wisdom.

"Trust your hunches. They're usually based on facts filed away just below the conscious level."

Joyce Brothers

Trusting yourself is crucial to everything; absolutely everything.

Trusting you'll do the right thing at the right time. Trusting you'll act with your best intentions.

Trusting your intuition. Trusting you'll make the best decision given the circumstances.

"Trust yourself, you know more than you think you do."

Benjamin Spock

Trusting yourself at all times.

> *"Trust your own instincts, go inside, follow your heart. Right from the start. Go ahead and stand up for what you believe in. As I've learned, that's the path to happiness."*

Lesley Ann Warren

Now that you've prepared yourself and you're in action, trusting yourself more will build your confidence, in you and your motivation to continue along your path.

Trusting others is essential, although it's often fraught with disappointment when others let you down.

We rely on others to be honest and truthful in their dealings with us.

We place our confidence and trust in others to treat us honorably and respectfully.

We place our trust in others through choosing to risk becoming vulnerable.

Trust is a complex concept.

> *"Trust your gut. You know yourself, so don't let somebody else tell you who you are."*

Tatiana Maslany

Often others let us down when they don't perform or behave in the way we've trusted them to.

Trust is critical to long-term relationships of any kind. Trust is a two-way street, almost like a dance between the two parties.

Trust takes time to build. Trust takes even more time to rebuild if it's been damaged or destroyed.

> "He who does not trust enough, will not be trusted."
>
> Lao Tzu

Your mindset affects your ability to trust you.

Trusting that you can maintain the momentum in your life and businesses creates sustainability and safety for you.

Let's explore ways you can deepen your trust of YOU.

12. Step 7: Your Truth

Oh NO!!! Not again!

"I've got a headache. You'll have to go and milk for me!" He shouted at me from the other room as soon as my morning alarm rang.

It happened so frequently it became the norm. I sank deeper and deeper into the mire that was my reality at the time. The repercussions of disobeying were just too great for me to consider enduring at the time. I felt within every cell of my body that my only choice was to obey him.

He was a classic and highly-skilled manipulative, controlling, lying, predator male who'd made sure I was totally removed from all contact with anyone who could support me. I was totally isolated; from friends, from family, from everyone. Disconnected, alone, isolated, lonely; at his beck and call every moment of every day. At his mercy; if I didn't obey and behave as he expected, the retaliations got worse and worse. I had no choice; I got up, dressed and went to do as he commanded.

What surprises me the most, as I reflect, is how deeply I had fallen into the well of despair. How totally isolated I'd become. How completely alone I felt. How much control he had over me.

I realize now I was disconnected from life, disconnected from people; and tragically, disconnected from myself!

Yet, despite everything, I clung onto a tiny thread of me.

Over time, that tiny thread became the rope I used to rise up and out of that deep, dark hole.

Climbing out was painful; excruciatingly so. Yet, all along there was a tiny glimmer of hope. The light at the end of the tunnel. The sky at the top of the well. And the thread of hope, gradually morphing into the rope that enabled me to rise. To get out. To break free.

Trust your Truth

> "You can't connect the dots looking forward; you can only connect them looking backwards. So you have to trust that the dots will somehow connect in your future. You have to trust in something – your gut, destiny, life, karma, whatever. This approach has never let me down, and it has made all the difference in my life."
>
> Steve Jobs

You know things no one else has ever known.

You possess a truth that no one else on the planet has.

You're living a life that no one else ever has lived.

Own what you know; know that you know what you know and be confident in that. Know that, what you've gone through in your life has prepared you to live the life you're living, and make the difference you dream of making, in this world.

When you're actively listening to your inner voice, you are more able to trust yourself.

*"Whoever is careless with the truth in small matters
cannot be trusted with important matters."*

Albert Einstein

Even when you've not listened in the past, as I hadn't. Even
when you've not always made the best decisions, as I didn't.
Even when you've not made courageous choices, as I
hadn't. Or even chosen consciously at all, as I wasn't. There
is a way out.

What I discovered is that climbing out took a substantial
amount of determination, as well as consistently tuning
into my inner voice and intuition to ensure I was on the
right track at every moment. I knew, without a shadow of
doubt, that I could no longer live my life in default; that
each choice I made needed to be a conscious, courageous
choice, and that every decision I made needed to be aligned
with my values, my vision and my mission.

I knew that I knew my truth, and I wasn't letting go of it.
I grew to trust myself more and more. As I trusted myself
more, that tiny thread transformed into the strong rope
that I used to rise up and out of that deep, dark and very
unpleasant hole.

*"Be true to yourself, stay focused and stay you, take
advice from other folks, use what you can, but never
mind what is not for you. For the most part, trust
yourself and believe in what you are doing."*

Musiq Soulchild

When you're not being who you truly are, when you're trying to be someone else; the person they expect you to be,

the person who keeps everyone else happy, then you're not being true to yourself. You're not owning your own truth. Essentially, you're lying to yourself. When that happens, you dilute your trust of yourself and you pollute how you view you.

In a practical sense, you're adding some muddy water to the filtered water you were planning to drink. When you allow that to happen, you then have to add lots of fresh water so that at some point you feel comfortable trusting you again. The fresh water is the effort it requires for you to rebuild your trust of you, which effectively you've broken by not being in your truth. By not showing up as who you truly are.

In contrast, when you have consciously chosen and decided to live your truth; the life you were born to live, then, you'll be able to trust that you'll do the right thing at the right time, trust you'll make the best decision given the circumstances and trust that you're acting with the best intentions.

> *"The hardest part when I decided to move into acting was trusting I'd made the right decision."*
>
> *Caitriona Balfe*

Trusting yourself, your gut and your intuition means you become more courageous and more confident. Making that decision is crucial; it will help you achieve your goals and realize your dreams. It's an important step in creating your path.

Word of warning: what can happen next frequently occurs without us even realizing. Whatever area of life you're making new choices in, this can happen. Truth is, it usually does, so listen up, as it will sneak up on you when you least expect.

Your subconscious, that part of you that works on autopilot, will pop you back into auto-mode and you'll find yourself taking actions that you'd have taken in the past but that you no longer want to. It does that because your subconscious wants to protect you.

Your subconscious naturally wants to keep you safe, and it perceives that by taking different actions you're putting yourself in the path of potential danger. So, it causes you to take your old auto-action steps; to do what you'd always have done in the past in a similar situation, even though you no longer wish to be doing it.

The secret here is to stop yourself as soon as you realize this is happening, turn yourself around, recommit to your new choice and take new action accordingly. That takes strength and courage; it can be scary and can cause you to doubt your new choices.

Maintaining your new course of action requires you to be vigilant and strong. Vigilant in observing yourself, and strong in keeping yourself on your new path.

Courage in action. Courage in being. Courage in living your truth. Courage in following your inner voice.

> "All you need is the plan, the road map, and the courage to press on to your destination."
>
> Earl Nightingale

Much of my life, I'd spent building and maintaining a protective shell round myself. A barricade between me and the world. To keep me safe. To protect me. Through a lifetime of longing to fit in somewhere, anywhere, I'd created my own safe place where no one could reach me. The problem with staying there was that when I'm hiding it's impossible for me to fulfil my mission in the world, that reason I'm alive.

What I came to realize is that being vulnerable; sharing more of me, sharing my truth, allows others to see me and enables my light to shine in the world. Vulnerability truly is perfect protection and being myself is safe.

> "You gain strength, courage and confidence by every experience in which you really stop to look fear in the face. You are able to say to yourself; I lived through this horror. I can take the next thing that comes along."
>
> Eleanor Roosevelt

That's why having your vision, your mission, your purpose, your goals and your vision board all displayed, so they are a reminder to you of why you're on this particular journey, makes trusting your truth easier.

I believe that we all know the right answers for us, and that leaning into our intuition and following its lead not only strengthens our resolve to continue on our desired path, but enhances our success.

> "As soon as you trust yourself, you will know how to live."
>
> Johan Wolfgang von Goeth

Chapter Summary

- Own your own truth and let it guide you.
- Listen to your intuition, that deep inner wisdom inside of you.
- Trusting your own inner truth allows you to be more courageous and more confident.
- Vulnerability is perfect protection.

Reflect

- When are you not listening to your intuition?
- Where in your life could you benefit from receiving answers from your intuition?

Implement

- Display your vision, your mission and your goals somewhere so they can inspire you more often.
- Create a juicy and inspirational vision board. There's more information about vision boards and a workshop to assist you in your resources here: https://daph-newells.com/decidebookdownloads/

13. Step 8: Mindset Matters

"I have the choice of being constantly active and happy or introspectively passive and sad."

Sylvia Plath

It all started when I stopped living in default mode. Then, and only then, was I able to grow on the inside. I'd owned and accepted that what was present in my life was because of my choices and decisions. I'd co-created it.

That was the day when I chose to step out of victim mentality to become my own hero. All my life, I'd heard excuses for why people's lives were less than ideal; I thought that way of thinking was normal. I didn't know any different; I didn't know there was another way.

When I finally realized I was totally responsible for what was showing up in my life, everything changed. The predator males showing up in my relationships with their controlling, manipulative, abusive muscles well-honed, were a direct result of my feelings of unworthiness. They were evidence that I didn't believe I was good enough for anyone or anything different.

The lack of abundance was a direct result of my scarcity mindset. That's how I'd been raised in my family of origin, where there was never enough of anything; and, so it was in my home also.

Until, I decided to change ME. Everything changed when I chose to step out of living in default mode and be my own hero. It all started with me calling time on letting life happen to me.

Truth is, it was a huge mindset shift for me, as it changed everything I'd been raised to believe and a lifetime of living in default mode.

> "Your mindset matters. It affects everything – from the business and investment decisions you make, to the way you raise your children, to your stress levels and overall well-being."
>
> Peter Diamandis

Your mindset matters. Your mindset is the ideas and attitudes with which you approach any and every situation. Your mindset matters because how you approach every situation directly influences the consequences.

> "You are a living magnet. What you attract into your life is in harmony with your dominant thoughts."
>
> Brian Tracy

Mindset matters. Mindset does matter.

> "From the neck up is where you win or lose the battle. It's the art of war. You have to lock yourself in and strategize your mindset."
>
> Anthony Joshua

Your attitude, your beliefs and your thoughts all determine your results. How you think about something affects your outcome. What you believe impacts everything in your life. What you think affects everything in your life.

> "*Anything is possible if you have the mindset and the will and desire to do it and put in the time.*"
>
> *Roger Clemens*

You get to choose. It's all up to you!

Who are you being?

> "*The only way you can be happy is if you be completely yourself. You have to be you. Don't be what you think you should be.*"
>
> *Afrojack*

You get to choose who you are, in each and every moment.

You get to choose your life. However, it's not just a case of wandering through the supermarket of life and picking from the shelf anything and everything you want. It's just not like that.

The first step in choosing your life, is choosing who you are being.

Who you are being is vital for everything in your life.

Who you are being impacts what you do.

Who you are being impacts what you have.

> "*Life is about being and becoming, not having and getting.*"

In every moment, you get to choose who you are being. Each and every moment of your life becomes a decision for you to make.

Who are you being now? Right now? Who will you be in five minutes? Who will you be in an hour from now? Who will you be this evening? Who will you be tomorrow?

If you're unhappy with what you have and what you are doing, you can change who you are being, and the results will alter accordingly.

Change who you are being to change your life. Choosing who you are being is not just a choice or a privilege. Choosing who you are being is your responsibility. Choosing who you are being is pretty much the first step. Are you ready for it?

> *"I think it's very important that you make your own decision about what you are. Therefore, you're responsible for your actions, so you don't blame other people."*
>
> *Prince William*

Be. Do. Have.

What if it's possible to be everything you ever dreamed of being?

What if it's possible to do everything you ever wanted to do?

What if it's also possible to have everything you ever imagined?

What if?

One important factor here is whether you believe it's possible. If you don't believe it's possible then you'll never be, do or have it. Period.

> "*Taking responsibility for your beliefs and judgments gives you the power to change them.*"
>
> *Byron Katie*

While we often know things, knowing isn't enough. If we don't believe them, truly and deeply believe them, then they can't possibly be true for us.

Another important factor here is the order of the process. What do I mean? So often we think we have to have, or do whatever, before we can be. And that's a totally screwed view.

> "*You've got to be before you can do and do before you can have.*"
>
> *Zig Ziglar*

Everything in life depends on being. Who you are being in any moment determines your outcome more than anything else; more than what you do and more than what you have.

What you do and what you have is a direct result of who you are being. The truth is, you can be, do and have absolutely anything and everything you could possibly desire, imagine or dream of. You absolutely can. It's up to you!

> *"To help yourself, you must be yourself. Be the best that you can be. When you make a mistake, learn from it, pick yourself up and move on."*
>
> Dave Pelzer

Do you love mornings? Or not so much?

What I know is that most people fit into one category or the other. They either love mornings, or they don't.

Me, I'm a morning person through and through. I remember as a child being sent back to bed regularly and told I wasn't allowed to get up till mum got up. I have absolutely no idea why, but that is what I remember!

I remember feeling frustrated and even grumpy because I was raring to go, champing at the bit, wanting to get into the new day, yet I wasn't allowed to! Nowadays, I go to the beach EVERY morning. I walk, I enjoy the solitude to connect and prepare for my day. I return home excited and ready for anything and everything the day may bring.

What I've learned is that how we start our day has a profound impact on how our day plays out. Which takes me back to my initial question, do you love mornings? And following on from that, how do you love to start your day?

Do you rise early and spend some YOU time before the rest of your household wakes? Or, do you sleep-in, enjoying every last minute in bed, and then rush round in a panic, frantically attempting to get organized?

Truth is, how you start your day impacts your day. Your results. Your feelings. How you relate to others. Your performance. Your outcomes. Your everything!!!

Taking YOU time so that YOU get to start your day in a way that prepares you well, is paramount to your success.

If you're a late riser, be really curious so that you find a way to begin your day that isn't in panic mode. Get really curious as to what you can prepare the night before and how you can set your day up to succeed before you go to bed.

When you're on a mission, as you are, this becomes even more important. What could you change in your morning routine so you can begin your day relaxed and prepared for whatever the day brings?

What would make it possible for you to take time for you in the mornings?

> *"Taking time for yourself is crucial when you're surrounded by people all day."*
>
> *Kaia Gerber*

The act of taking time out for you shows that you value yourself.

> *"You shouldn't feel guilty about taking time for yourself. Every so often, everyone needs to give themselves a big ol' bear hug and treat themselves to some TLC."*
>
> *Sean Covey*

Is your Pot Big Enough?

Are you growing?

Some time ago, I was busily creating my new garden. And it was bringing me sooooooo much joy! Finally, I was up to the part of creating my new garden that included planting lots of plants, shrubs and trees. Some of them had been given to me a couple of years earlier and had been waiting in pots for me to build the necessary retaining walls so I could plant them.

They were in large pots; tubs really, and they'd grown into substantial plants accordingly. When I went to plant them, it seemed they didn't want to leave their pots. I'd talked to them, telling them how excited I was to be planting them into their permanent homes at last. And how they'd be able to grow even bigger without the walls of their tub constraining them.

They either didn't hear me or they didn't understand what I meant or they simply just didn't care. Apparently, they sure didn't want to leave their tubs in a hurry. They were locked in there, glued in there; they were attached in some way that was extremely difficult for me to separate them from the tub they were in.

It ended up being a huge mission separating them from their pot so I could plant them in their new home. Finally, I did win. And they were happily planted in my new garden. I'm guessing they're happy. They certainly are behaving as though they're content. They're flowering away merrily, enjoying our lovely spring weather here as I write this.

And I just know they're going to grow even faster now they

are able to expand their root base as much as they choose to without their tub walls constraining them.

And it got me thinking, that it's like that for us sometimes. We get comfortable and we become content, and sometimes that makes us resist change, like my trees resisting being removed from their pots.

Truth is that often our pot has become too small for us, as it had for my trees. When that happens, we need to jump from our small pot into a larger context so we can grow into the women we are destined to become.

Often, we find that scary, and choose to remain cramped in our current pots avoiding growth; choosing to remain in our comfort zone. Most times, we benefit from having some support when we move into our larger context; when we're living life at the edge!

When will you finally let the 'real you' out?

For many years, I wasn't being 'me'. Truth is, I didn't even know who 'me' was for a lot of that time. I just knew that I wasn't happy being who I was being. I wasn't content or joyful. I wasn't being truthful to myself; I wasn't respecting myself.

I was aware that I wasn't being the real me. I was being who I thought everyone expected me to be. Being who they wanted me to be. Behaving how I thought I was meant to. Keeping others happy. Doing what was expected of me. Keeping quiet when every part of me wanted to shout out and say what I felt needed to be said. It seemed easier at the time.

And all the while I was receiving the message that I wasn't good enough. That I couldn't be who I wanted to be. That I couldn't be any different to who I was being. That I didn't deserve any more. That I wasn't valuable. That I wasn't valued. That I wasn't anyone special. I was just like everyone else.

But I wasn't. I was me. I'm unique. There's only one of me. Forever; I'm the only one of me. I have a gift to share with the world that no one else can give. I have a role to play in our world and society that no one else can fulfill. Truth is, you do too.

What's more, if I don't follow my passion and live my life on purpose then it's not only me that misses out, it's also all the people who I'm here to serve and help.

So, I'm on a mission. I'm ruthlessly committed to doing what matters to me and to the people I'm here to serve and support. I'm committed to *inspiriting* women to BE their best self in every sphere of life and business, to creating a life and business truly tailor-made to fit their uniqueness, so they can make a difference and make money; to blossom courageously. Nothing will stop me. I'm totally committed.

How about you? Are you being the 'real you'? What are you committed to?

> "Whether you think you can or think you can't, you're right."
>
> *Henry Ford*

Value You

"You can put someone in a new home, but you can't give them a new mindset."

Dan Phillips

When you recognize your own value and appreciate you; yourself, you show up differently. It changes who you are being.

Recognizing your own value, both as a person and the contribution you bring to the world, is paramount to establishing a positive mindset and protecting your mindset. When you know and own your own value. When you get your own significance as a person you are then able to stand in courage, owning your unique place in the world.

Valuing and appreciating YOU enables you to truly be who you are born to be. You are then in a stronger position to contribute to the world in your unique way, and make the difference you are on this planet to make.

When I finally got this concept, my feeling of never fitting in anywhere didn't matter anymore. Diddlysquat. Just never even entered my thinking anymore. The difference was that finally I fitted ME.

One young lady, a rising corporate leader, who I was coaching, felt as though she had to conform to how her male managers expected her to show up and who they expected her to be. Through coaching with me, she was able to appreciate her own value more and more, and show up truly as her. On one occasion, as a result of working with me, she had a courageous conversation with her manager, which resulted in him respecting her more, valuing her more and giving her a large salary increase.

No one can do it for you. It's all up to YOU. Changing your mindset is not a one-time done and dusted thing. Your mindset matters. It's really important.

Your mindset requires maintenance regularly. What you think about and give thanks about is what you'll bring about.

Positive Perspective

> "I'm a very positive person. My grandmother taught me that happiness is both a skill and a decision, and you are responsible for the outcome."
>
> Helen McCrory

Choose and decide to see everything positively.

Today, we take it for granted that we have light bulbs. Thomas Edison is famous for inventing the light bulb. Edison tried thousands of attempts before he succeeded. After around 700 unsuccessful attempts, a reporter for the New York Times asked Edison how it felt to have failed 700 times. Edison answered:

> "I have not failed seven hundred times. I have not failed once. I have succeeded in proving that those seven hundred ways will not work. When I have eliminated all the ways that will not work, I will find the way that will work".

Edison went on to successfully illuminate the world and make it a safer place. He changed how we live our lives because we can now have light whenever we choose.

"My dad encouraged us to fail. Growing up, he would ask us what we failed at that week. If we didn't have something, he would be disappointed. It changed my mindset at an early age that failure is not the outcome, failure is not trying. Don't be afraid to fail."

Sara Blakely

There is no such thing as failure, only feedback. Failures are opportunities to learn. Mistakes are opportunities to learn. Choose to learn the lesson and keep failing forward; keep on trying. Keep moving forward toward your goal, learning vital lessons as you progress.

Attitude of Gratitude

"Today's gratitude buys tomorrow's happiness."

Michael McMillan

One of the single most important things you can do to cement your new positive mindset, is to make a practice of reflecting on all the good things in your life.

As you say thank you to life, God, the Universe, or whatever you feel most comfortable with and connected to, you are cultivating your attitude of gratitude which is a direct opposite of a negative mindset and victim mentality.

Writing it down.

Vocalizing it.

Out loud or internally.

The choice is yours.

The important thing is to do it.

Writing down what you're grateful for in a gratitude journal can be very uplifting and encouraging to reflect on.

Affirmations

Stretch your comfort zone and maintain your positive mindset by bombarding your mind with new thoughts and images of all your goals, as if they were already complete.

> *"I've always believed in magic. When I wasn't doing anything in this town, I'd go up every night, sit in Mulholland Drive, look out at the city, stretch out my arms and say, "Everybody wants to work with me. I'm a really good actor. I have all kinds of great movie offers." I'd just repeat these things over and over, literally convincing myself that I had a couple of movies lined up. I'd drive up that hill, ready to take the world on, going "Movie offers are out there for me, I just don't hear them yet." It was like total affirmations, antidotes to the stuff that stems from my family background."*
>
> *Jim Carrey (from an interview in Movieline, July 1994)*

An affirmation is a statement that describes a goal in its already completed state. Make your affirmations super effective in these ways:

- Start with "I (insert your name) am"
- Use present tense – as if you have it NOW
- Use only positive words
- Keep it brief

- Be specific
- Include a verb ending in -ing
- Include at least one emotion, or feeling word
- Make it all about YOU
- Add in "or something better"

Review your affirmations at least once every day. Read them. Write them. Listen to them. See them. Do whichever you decide, just do it.

Journaling

Writing on paper. Your thoughts. Your feelings. Your dreams. Your aspirations. Your vision. Your mission. Your purpose. Your passion.

Journaling is free flow writing in which you can:

- Reflect
- Go deep into your own thoughts and feelings
- Write about what excites you
- Write about what interests you
- Write about what scares you
- Get it all out of your head and onto paper

Journaling takes time that is definitely hugely beneficial for you. It's important to write your journal by hand on paper. Putting pen to paper slows you down. It allows your thoughts and feelings to flow.

Journaling helps you focus on what you want, by dedicating time to focus on your dreams and desires, and record them.

Journaling is a fabulous idea-incubator and dream-catcher,

as it helps you flesh out your dreams and ideas and gives them shape and being.

> *"In my journal I do not just express myself more openly than I would do to any person; I create myself."*

> *Susan Sontag*

Just five minutes of dedicated journaling time every day will make a difference in your life.

> *"What marks you out is having the mindset of a champion."*

> *Manu Bennett*

Changing your mindset will change your results. Maintaining your mindset is a daily practice which strengthens your courage to be who you were born to be.

> *"Whatever the mind can conceive and believe, it can achieve."*

> *Napoleon Hill*

Taking care of your mindset and maintaining a positive mindset are important elements to ensuring you stay on your chosen path. Strengthening your mindset will strengthen your belief in YOU and your ability to make the best decision, based on the information you have at any time.

> *"Success is really about your mindset."*

> *F. Gary Gray*

Chapter Summary

- You choose your mindset, every moment.
- Who you are being is your choice and makes a difference to everything.
- Choose and decide to see everything positively.
- Failure is merely feedback.
- Choose to have an attitude of gratitude.
- Harness the power of affirmations.
- Create YOU and your life through journaling.
- Changing and maintaining a positive mindset will change your results.
- YOUR mindset matters.

Reflect

- Which of your thoughts, beliefs and attitudes would it benefit you to change?
- Where are you still playing the blame game?
- What adjustments to your morning routine would better set you up to succeed each day?

Implement

- Keep a gratitude journal.
- Keep moving towards your goal.
- Incorporate affirmations into your daily practices.
- Journal regularly.

14. Step 9: Sustainability

Tootle is now training to be a flyer on the main trunk railway. And he's going for it. Faster and faster. Then one day;

A dreadful thing happened.

He looked across the meadow he was running through and saw a fine, strong black horse.

"Race you to the river," shouted the black horse, and kicked up his heels.

Away went the horse. His black tail streamed out behind him, and his mane tossed in the wind. Oh, how he could run!

"Here I go," said Tootle to himself. "If I am going to be a Flyer, I can't let a horse beat me," he puffed. "Everyone at school will laugh at me."

His wheels turned so fast that they were silver streaks. The cars lurched and bumped together. And just as Tootle was sure he could win, the tracks made a great curve.

"Oh, Whistle!" cried Tootle. "That horse will beat me now. He'll run straight while I take the Great Curve."

Then the Dreadful Thing happened.

After all that Bill had said about Staying on the Rails No Matter What, Tootle jumped off the tracks and raced alongside the black horse!

You've got this thing going. Trucking along. The next thing

to think about is whether what you've created in your life is capable of being maintained at a steady level without exhausting your resources.

For Tootle, practicing staying on the rails no matter what was not sustainable when the threat of the horse beating him to the river loomed. At that moment, in Tootle's mind, avoiding losing the race and averting the risk of his school mates teasing him was more important than staying on the rails no matter what.

Sustainability is about whether you're able to stay in momentum without too much effort, without it being hard work. If it's repeatable, then it's generally sustainable.

Can you keep going at your current pace ad infinitum? Without giving up? Without falling down?

Are you able to sustain your current momentum without too much effort?

As you grow, can you keep growing without putting in heaps more work?

Systems give you Freedom

"Serving the world's best cheese rolls since 1955."

Yes, we did.

"Delivering beautiful food to you."

Yes, we did, and very good at it we were too, according to our customers, both in the café and at functions where we catered. I'd purchased the business as a going concern, having been assured all the systems required were already in place. What I discovered was a completely different story.

Each staff member had been assigned particular tasks to perform every day. It was all listed on a chart on the wall. That was the system! Didn't work too well in practice. No one knew what anyone else actually did! No one took responsibility for another's tasks when they had a day off, were sick or on vacation.

For a system to be sustainable, it requires that anyone can follow the procedure laid out, and perform the task effectively.

It's important to become sustainable if you want to continue without exhausting yourself or your resources.

Systematize everything you can to support the scalability of your business. Systemize everything you can at home to support your family having time for enjoying life and having fun.

Have the ball rolling. Keep the ball rolling. Maybe it's slowing down and needs help to speed it up.

Staying in momentum, consistently and constantly taking action, is easier to maintain than stopping and starting again.

One person doing all the chores at home is not sustainable. Creating systems for tasks means they happen with less effort. Perhaps you could:

- Have everyone take their laundry to the appropriate place and sort it when they leave it so it's easy to see

when a load needs to be started
- Compile a roster for emptying the dishwasher
- Hire a cleaner or create a system to spread the responsibility
- Put a blank list on the fridge for everyone to add to as they notice pantry items that need replaced
- Hold family meetings regularly to discuss making these systems more effective for everyone to spread the responsibility and enable family members to better support one another

A roller coaster ride at work is not sustainable. Creating systems and procedures creates structure and frees up time and resources. Documenting how you do things is a great way to start this process. Ensure the systems you create support you and your vision. Create a library of templates for routine communications, such as for sending out quotes or estimates.

Systems provide you with a viable, credible, continuous, renewable way of solving a problem.

Repeatable systems beat doing everything piecemeal, hands down.

Rhythms and Patterns

> "The first rule of sustainability is to align with natural forces."
>
> Paul Hawken

Days of the week. Months of the year. The seasons. Cycles of the moon. Day and night. Rhythms and patterns are everywhere.

Rhythms and patterns are present in all parts of your life. Recognizing them, appreciating them, understanding them and honoring them helps you handle the ebbs and flows of life.

Listen to your body. Rest when you need to rest. Sleep when you need to sleep. Exercise when you need to move. Feed your body regularly.

Get familiar with the rhythms and patterns of your family and your work life.

School holidays, while busier in the café, were quieter for catering for me, all those years ago.

Get familiar with your busiest times of the year, of the day, of the week, of the month. Know your quiet times.

Dig deep to discover the rhythms and patterns in your life. Use that knowledge to enhance the sustainability of your life.

Time Out

Ensuring that you take time out is part of your daily experience. Having a break from routine is essential to your well-being.

Taking time to smell the roses is important. To wander through your garden discovering the new buds, flowers and perfumes; noticing the fruits and vegetables nearly ready to harvest. Not to just always work whenever you're in your garden!

Many of us believe we're too busy to take time out. The

truth is, however, that taking time out will refresh you so that you are more productive as a result of taking time out.

Leaving your office building for your lunch break. Leaving your desk for your coffee. Leaving your phone in your pocket or handbag when you're with your family, friends or colleagues.

Even though I enjoy beach time every morning, I often find myself there through the day as well. What I find is that even ten minutes spent on the beach will revive me and energize me. Taking time out at the beach repays me in increased productivity.

In the days that followed Tootle tying his race with the horse, he became fond of playing in the meadow and not staying on the rails.

Tootle looked at the meadow. It was full of buttercups.

"It's like a big yellow carpet. How I should like to play in them and hold one under my searchlight to see if I like butter!" thought Tootle.

His wheels began to say over and over again, "Do you like butter? Do you?"

"I don't know," said Tootle crossly. "But I'm going to find out."

He danced around and around and held one of the buttercups under his searchlight.

"I do like butter!" cried Tootle. "I do!"

Next day Tootle played all day in the meadow. He watched a green frog and he made a daisy chain. He found a rain barrel and he said softly: "Toot!"

"TOOT!" shouted the barrel.

"Why I sound like a flyer already!" cried Tootle.

Engage Others

Ask for support and help.

Receive it with thanks.

Bill quickly discovers what Tootle has been doing. Not wanting to take away Tootle's chance at becoming a Flyer, Bill asks for and receives support.

He concocts a plan with the mayor of Lower Trainswitch to put Tootle back on the tracks.

Bill ran from one store to the next, buying ten yards of this and twenty yards of that and all you have of the other. The Chief Oiler and the First, Second and Third Assistant Oilers were hammering and sawing instead of oiling and polishing.

And Tootle? Well Tootle was in the meadow watching the butterflies flying and wishing he could dip and soar as they did.

Not a store in Lower Trainswitch was open the next day and not a person was at home. By the time the sun came up, every villager was hiding in the meadow along the tracks. And each of them had a red flag. It had taken all the red goods in Lower Trainswitch, and hard work by the Oilers, but there was a red flag for everyone.

Tootle playing happily in the meadow day after day was not sustainable. Nor was playing in the meadow moving him toward his goal of becoming a Famous Flyer. Bill asked for support from the Mayor of Lower Trainswitch, all the Oilers and all the residents of Lower Trainswitch. They all willingly gave their support.

Asking for and receiving support and help is a sign of strength. A key point to realize here is that your greatest indicator of success is your capacity to ASK.

Do what falls in your zone of genius, that which brings you most joy and is where you shine.

Make it Yours

No one size fits all. We can't fit in a box; nor do we benefit from trying to!

Sustainability for your life will look different to anyone else's.

> *"To me, a leader is someone who holds her- or himself accountable for finding potential in people and processes. And so what I think is really important is sustainability."*
>
> *Brene Brown*

The rhythms and patterns of your life are unique to you.

That said, seek support and a listening ear to guide you as you create sustainable solutions for you.

Chapter Summary

- Systems create freedom and sustainability.
- Respect the rhythms and patterns present in your life.
- Take time out regularly.
- Ask for and receive support.
- Stop doing what you don't love doing.
- Become sustainable so that you can grow toward your desired vision without exhausting either yourself or your resources, or both.

Reflect

- Can you keep going at your current pace, ad infinitum?
- What systems could you improve or implement in your life?
- What does refreshing time-out mean to you?
- Who can you ask for support?

Implement

- Identify the rhythms and patterns in your life.
- Create systems that support you.
- Identify tasks or roles to delegate.

15. Pillar 4: Hero

> "Heroes are never perfect, but they're brave, they're authentic, they're courageous, determined, discreet and they've got grit."
>
> Wade Davis

A hero is a person endowed with great strength or ability.

> "A hero is no braver than an ordinary man, but he is brave five minutes longer."
>
> Ralph Waldo Emerson

A hero shows great courage.

> "A hero is somebody who voluntarily walks into the unknown."
>
> Tom Hanks

A hero is admired for achievements and noble qualities.

> "Hard times don't create heroes. It is during the hard times when the 'hero' within us is revealed."
>
> Bob Riley

A hero is regarded as a role model or ideal by others.

> "A hero is someone who has given his or her life to something bigger than oneself."
>
> Joseph Campbell

A hero is the principal character in their own life, they take the lead, they initiate and maintain leadership of self.

"Everybody is a hero in their own story."

Maeve Binchy

Once upon a time, not so long ago, I became my own hero, my own knight in shining armor, and rescued ME.

I'd waited long enough for a 'real' hero, a real 'knight in shining armor', to come and rescue me. You know, the fairy-story kind.

Pretty soon it became obvious nothing would change unless I became my own hero and rescued ME. No one else was going to do it. Despite all the fairy-tales I'd read, there was no handsome prince going to come to save me and take care of me. It was up to me.

> *"A hero is somebody who is selfless, who is generous in spirit, who just tries to give back as much as possible and help people. A hero to me is someone who saves people and who really deeply cares."*

Debi Mazar

Without doubt, rescuing ME, being my own hero, has proved harder for me to do than rescuing others. It took guts and courage, strength and focus.

I had to prepare for it.

I had to take action.

I had to trust.

> "A *hero is someone who understands the responsibility that comes with freedom.*"

> Bob Dylan

Dictionary.com says entrepreneurs are our modern heroes.

> "A *hero is an ordinary individual who finds the strength to persevere and endure in spite of overwhelming obstacles.*"

> Christopher Reeve

As parents, you become heroes for your children. Entrepreneurs and business owners become heroes for your clients.

It's up to you to look after you so that you can better serve and support those who look up to you.

Heroes in movies and stories are always well looked after by those who look up to them.

Heroes are more heroic when they have community, connection, collaboration and support.

> "*Together we can change the world, just one random act of kindness at a time.*"

> Ron Hall

Heroes are heroes just by being themselves and letting the real them shine through.

16. Step 10: Champion

"I am the master of my fate; I am the captain of my soul."

William Ernest Henley

A champion is someone who defends a person or a cause.

Here, we are looking at how you can champion you; how you can support and defend YOU. If you're an alchemist like me, you're a natural at championing others. For many of us, especially women, championing ourselves is a whole different story, which means we need to purposefully seek ways for you to champion YOU.

"Nobody can go back and start a new beginning, but anyone can start today and make a new ending."

Maria Robinson

Kick your inner critic to the curb!

You know it well! It's that voice that keeps speaking to you. Criticizing you. Putting you down.

Causing you to doubt yourself. How many times every day does your inner critic win?

Every time you listen to your inner critic, it wins. Every time you take notice of what your inner critic says, it wins. Every moment you're influenced by your inner critic, it wins. Whenever you pay attention to your inner critic, it wins.

Truth is, when you listen to your inner critic, it's impossible for you to champion you. When you let your inner critic win, you make everything more difficult than it needs to be.

In every moment, you get to choose. Will you listen to your inner critic? Or will you kick your inner critic to the curb and courageously step onward?

Flipping the switch to quiet your inner critic and appreciate your uniqueness is life-changing.

Living life on your terms requires you to appreciate who you truly are.

Addicted to chocolate, stressed and doubting her every move after several setbacks, Lorna (not her real name), felt caught in a downward spiral. Although her business appeared successful on the outside, she was feeling any-thing but successful when she called me. Frustrated, over-whelmed and self-critical, her life was full, busily tending to the needs of others. After coaching with me, Lorna no longer sacrifices herself to keep her clients happy; she's championing herself and being the hero of her own life.

Truth is, minutes are more important than hours. Hours are more important than days. Time's ticking along. It's the little things. The choices that you make each and every moment change the outcome for you. Are you willing to kick your inner critic to the curb? To be done with listening to it? It took more than one swift kick for Lorna to quiet her inner critic, she found my support invaluable on each step of her journey.

Are you ready to choose in every moment who you will be, without listening to your inner critic?

"Go confidently in the direction of your dreams. Live the life you have imagined."

Henry David Thoreau

Be your own champion. Do it your way. Be you. The you that you know you're meant to be. Not the you that everyone else wants you to be.

Tootle was happily doing it his way; Tootle was being himself. By not allowing the horse to win the race to the river, Tootle discovered the joy of playing in the meadow, chasing butterflies, wishing he could dip and soar as they can, watching frogs and making daisy chains. He thought about all the fun he was enjoying playing in the meadow, as he passed his nights in the roundhouse.

How often do you 'should' on yourself?

I used to. A lot! Tootle did too. He told himself that he should stay on the rails no matter what and determined that:

"Tomorrow I will work hard. I will not even think of leaving the rails, no matter what."

And, so do a lot of the women I speak to.

Turns out we're good at it. Why do we do it? For me and for many others, it's because we never feel like we've done enough.

So, we 'should' on ourselves. 'I should have done', 'I should be finished', 'I should have made more'. And on and on we go. 'Shoulding' ourselves in the foot. Guilt-tripping ourselves.

Does it help? It sure never helped me. I was so hard on myself. I was my worst boss ever. I 'beat myself up' whenever I didn't seem to 'get it right', when things didn't work out the way I'd hoped; whatever it was, whatever right was. I did it.

And, you know what? It didn't help me one little bit. Truth is, it hindered me way more than it helped me.

I didn't realize it at the time. I was too involved. Too far in. Too deep in my dark hole. My doing place. My 'shoulding' place. I couldn't see the forest for the trees.

Here's the truth I came to realize. The way to achieve more is to appreciate every bit of progress you make. No matter how small and insignificant it seems. Champion you, at every possible moment.

Be grateful for everything. Even when bad stuff happens, as it does, look for and be grateful for the lessons it teaches you. Then let it go and move on to the better stuff that's waiting for you.

> "As we let our light shine, we unconsciously give other people permission to do the same. As we are liberated from our own fear, our presence actually liberates others."
>
> Marian Williamson

My role in life is to motivate and support women to be courageous, so they can withstand the shoulda, coulda, wouldas that come their way every day. And to serve and support them in deleting; 'I should have', 'I ought to have', and 'I could have' from thought and language.

When you champion YOU, you're able to champion others in your life, and to fully serve and support them heroically.

> *"Be yourself. Above all, let who you are, what you are, what you believe shine through every sentence you write, every piece you finish."*
>
> John Jakes

When you let your light shine, others are naturally attracted to you and you're able to serve and support them more. Then you become the candle to the moths; the honey pot to the bees.

> *"We are told to let our light shine, and if it does, we won't need to tell anybody it does. Lighthouses don't fire cannons to call attention to their shining – they just shine."*
>
> Dwight L Moody

Chapter Summary

- Kick your inner critic to the curb.
- Stop 'shoulding' on you.
- Be Yourself.
- Champion YOU.

Reflect

- What characteristics do you value in YOU?
- When will you stop listening to your inner critic?
- When will you stop 'shoulding' on you?

Implement

- Write down three things you're grateful for every day.
- Write down three things you value about yourself every day.
- Remove 'should' from your vocabulary, pinch yourself whenever you try to say it till not saying it becomes your new normal.

17. Step 11: Selfless Self-care

"Self-love, my liege, is not so vile a sin, as self-neglecting."

William Shakespeare

Self-care is selfless.

"You can search throughout the entire universe for someone who is more deserving of your love and affection than you are yourself, and that person is not to be found anywhere. You yourself, as much as anybody in the entire universe deserve your love and affection."

Buddha

Tending to your own well-being empowers you to better serve and support others; and therefore, is not concerned with your own selfish interests.

"If you don't love yourself, you can't love anybody else. And I think as women we really forget that."

Jennifer Lopez

When you care for and love yourself first you are truly able to love and care for others; it's like putting on your own oxygen mask first so you stay alive to care for the other person.

In practicing loving and caring for myself more, I've noticed I'm stronger within myself when I do and not so when I get busy and forget. That said, I've many years of not caring for nor loving myself. I've been there ... I've done it ... I've got the T-shirt. I've been oh-so-very-tired of working all the time and not having a life! Running on empty!

A few years ago, I was working my then biz from my home. I was working way too many hours. While my children were at school. After school I was busily running children round to all their after-school activities – doing the 'Mum' thing.

Evenings were spent working with clients and some Saturdays. Sunday was catch-up day; catching up at home, the garden, housework and spending time with my children.

Don't get me wrong here. I loved what I was doing. I loved my work with a passion. And, my clients loved it too. It was a mutual love-love thing going on. I loved being a mum too. Loved all that I did for my children. Loved all the time I spent with them.

Then I hit a brick wall and the bus got me all at the same time. I literally couldn't do anything. I was no use to anyone. No use to my children, my clients, or me. Anyone. Yes, I still did stuff for my home and my children. But that was it. And boy, was it a struggle.

I didn't know where to find help. I didn't know who could help me. It was a very scary time for me. I felt so alone and out of control. I still had to support my family. I desperately needed to find a way out of the deep hole I was stuck in. I didn't know what to do.

I feel sad all over again every time I hear of someone who is where I was. And that's why I've dedicated myself to helping others avoid the trauma and heartache I went through, digging my way out of the deep hole I'd become stuck in.

> "*Self-love requires you to be honest about your current choices and thought patterns and undertake new practices that reflect self-worth.*"
>
> *Caroline Kirk*

Here's the truth I came to realize, and it took me a very long time to realize it, to be totally honest.

The way to achieve more is to work less. And the way to achieve more is to care for yourself FIRST. YES, I know that's hard for you to hear. We women are so used to caring for everyone else first that you forget to look after yourself. We need to become our first priority. Then and only then will we be giving to everyone else from our overflow, rather than draining our cup.

> "*I love myself for I am a beloved child of the universe and the universe lovingly takes care of me now.*"
>
> *Louise Hay*

The Bible says it like this, "*Love your neighbor as you love yourself*" (Mark 12:31). I was brought up to that tune. Treating everyone else really, really well. I was loving my neighbor; I was not loving me. Part of that upbringing and biblical teaching tells us that if we focus on us, you focusing on you and me focusing on me, then we're being selfish and egotistical. It's a major contradiction that means we have to unlearn what we've been brought up to do and learn a new way of being; one that cares for one's self.

Truth is, we're being set up to fail. We're taught to do something and then told not to do it. What I know, now, is that until you love and accept yourself nothing else works. Nothing. Without self-love, self-care becomes yet another tick box in an overly busy life. Without self-love, no amount of self-care will fill us up.

Until we're full of self-love we'll be constantly giving to others from our fumes. When we're full of self-love, we're able to give from our overflow. Then we're truly able to love others. Then we're truly able to serve and support them as we feel called to.

The moral of the story is that self-love and self-care are essential for our well-being. For our very existence. Self-love and self-care are selfless, NOT selfish.

That said, we've been conditioned since we were children to believe it is selfish. As a result, we as women don't do a great job of looking after ourselves. Fact is, for many of us, our self-care sucks.

We're great at looking after everyone else. We care for our homes. We run after our partners and our children. We care for our extended family and our friends. We're constantly running around after, and caring for, everyone else. And our bucket is empty. Our well is dry. When Amelia came to me her bucket was empty and her well was dry; she'd been giving from nothing for a very long time. Truth is, we can't truly look after others unless we're looking after ourselves. Yet we keep trying.

Here's the secret remedy for this. Self-care has to be your top priority. As a business owner. As a mother. As a wife or partner. As a daughter. As a friend. As a woman. As a service provider.

> *"There are days I drop words of comfort on myself like falling leaves and remember that it is enough to be taken care of by myself."*
>
> Brian Andreas

Let's get into the nitty gritty here. What is self-care? Self-care is care provided for you, by you. It's about taking time each day to enjoy some activities that nurture you.

Self-care is about recognizing your own needs and taking steps to meet them. It includes any intentional activities you take to care for your physical, mental and emotional health. Self-care is taking great care of yourself and treating yourself with as much kindness as you do others.

Self-care is like the oxygen mask that drops down in front of you on an airplane. The first rule is that you put on your own oxygen mask before helping anyone else. Unless you do, you and your family could die before you help them to put their mask on. The message here is that only when you look after yourself are you able to effectively look after others. We get it when we're told on the airplane, but not in real life! The truth is that the same principle applies in real life.

Caring for yourself is the most important thing you can do for yourself and for others.

Unfortunately, it's also one of the easiest things to overlook when we're busy.

"It's not your job to like me … it's MINE!"

Byron Katie

Truth is, it's not only you who benefits from self-care but all the other people in your life benefit also.

Self-care is the constant repetition of many tiny activities and habits that together comfort you and ensure you're thriving and flourishing emotionally, physically and mentally. It's letting yourself do whatever you want to do; stuff that's fun for you.

Self-care for women is super important because we spend so much of our lives caring for others. When we don't take care of ourselves, we become stressed, exhausted and burned out. And that's when we feel like we're running on empty with nothing left to give. And that's why it's vital that we take time for self-care, to look after our self.

So, what does self-care look like? A myriad of possibilities in a practical sense. And the fabulous news is that it doesn't have to cost a lot of money and it doesn't have to take a lot of time, unless you choose for it to. We just need to do it. Often. Regularly. Intentionally.

Here's some ideas to get you started:

- Start a gratitude journal; list three things each day that you're grateful for
- Sit outside and listen to the birds or watch clouds
- Get enough sleep
- Take a 60-second break; close your eyes and just be, or look at a picture that inspires you
- Take another route to work, or another mode of

transport
- Listen to your favorite music
- Have a good laugh
- Take a quick nap
- Imagine you're your best friend, look yourself in the mirror and tell yourself how wonderful you are
- Ask three good friends to tell you what they love about you
- Spend time alone doing something that nourishes you such as reading or visiting a museum or art gallery
- Take a long bath or shower and afterwards relax in your robe, reading magazines
- Try yoga
- Take a walk or a run or climb stairs
- Do something just because it makes you happy
- Be still and be aware of your breathing
- Go to the park and play on the swings
- Run and play at the beach; splash and paddle in the waves
- Skip
- Throw or kick a ball

Essentially, self-care is about taking time out of your normal routine to spend time doing whatever you choose. For you. You're not trying to please anyone else. In fact, the moment you start to do that, it's not self-care any more.

Self-care is about being in the moment. And enjoying it.

> "*Whatever you are doing, love yourself for doing it. Whatever you are feeling, love yourself for feeling it.*"
>
> *Thaddeus Golas*

Little and often is all it takes for self-care to become a natural part of your life. By nurturing yourself with self-care, you'll feel more connected to both yourself and the world around you. You'll delight in small pleasures.

The truth is, we spend so much time in the if-onlys and the whens: *I'll feel better if ... I'll be happy when ...*

The more we enjoy the moment; the more we enjoy being our self in each moment, the more content we will be. And that's essentially what self- care is.

Remembering to care for yourself is hugely important for us as women. It'll help you shift from just functioning to flourishing. Only by caring for yourself can you really care for others.

Practicing exquisite self-love every day is an essential requirement in my life. Realizing that was a life-changing moment for me. I'd been brought up to care for everyone else. To serve everyone else. To support everyone else. To keep doing for others. With little or no thought for me or my needs.

And so it was. Year in. Year out. No wonder I kept burning out. Little surprise I often felt down and depressed.

When I'd decided I'd had enough, I sought advice and implemented a self-care plan. I made caring for me a priority. I infiltrated my days with acts of self-care.

For the longest time, I didn't feel it was making a difference. But, because I respected the people whose advice I'd taken, I kept going. Doing more.

After a while, I became aware that self-care was another tick-box on my already busy to-do list each day. I felt as though it was just another thing I had to do each day. And doing it didn't seem to be making a huge difference for me. I started putting even more fun activities in the mix. I added even more self-care.

What I came to realize was, there is another layer to this whole self-care thing that had never occurred to me. That deeper layer is all about self-love. Loving me. And loving me felt wrong. Difficult. Inappropriate. For so many reasons. For so long.

What I've learned is that loving me exquisitely each and every day is not only desirable, it's totally, vitally essential to my well-being.

> "Plant your own garden and decorate your own soul, instead of waiting for others to bring you flowers."
>
> Veronica A Shoffstall

Me loving me is what allows me to show up as me. Me loving me is what allows me to serve and support others. Me loving me is what allows me to be who I'm meant to be. Choosing to love me each and every moment of every day has surprised me beyond belief. It frees me to be me. Learning to love me has proven to be the biggest and most surprising lesson of all.

Self-love means you respect YOU. You have a positive self-image and you accept yourself unconditionally. Needless to say, it does not mean being arrogant, conceited or think-ing you are better than anyone else. It means you have a healthy regard for yourself, knowing that you are a worthy and valuable human being.

> "Loving yourself...does not mean being self-absorbed or narcissistic, or disregarding others. Rather it means welcoming yourself as the most honored guest in your own heart, a guest worthy of respect, a lovable companion."

> Margo Anand

> "It is never too late to be what you might have been."

> George Eliot

As Dr Clarissa Pinkola Estes says:

> "Be the first, be the last, be the best, be the only."

Chapter Summary

- Tend to yourself first.
- Love you first.
- Put on your own oxygen mask first.
- Make self-care a daily practice so you can truly serve and support others.
- Self-care is NOT selfish.

Reflect

- What would your life be like if YOU were your top priority?
- What would ideal self-care be for you?
- What are you grateful for about YOU?
- What do you love about YOU?

Implement

- Make a list of self-care ideas that enthuse you, and use it daily.
- Schedule appointments for YOU to do whatever you choose and then choose from your list what you'll do.
- In your gratitude journal, every day write three or more things you are grateful for about YOU, and three or more things you love about YOU.

18. Step 12: Community of Connection

"Alone we can do so little, together we can do so much."

Helen Keller

Sylvia (not her real name), felt isolated, overwhelmed and unappreciated when we first met. Leading a diverse team, feeling pulled in many different directions and being responsible for the overall running of a branch wasn't feeling at all rewarding for her. There were issues in her team and in the organization's hierarchy which contributed to what had become a very negative experience for Sylvia.

She was at a crossroad, unsure whether to stay or go. Through her regular coaching sessions with me, Sylvia grew to trust herself more and listen to her intuition. Slowly, things around her transformed. She believed in herself, had courageous conversations, grew in confidence and was recognized with an award from her employer.

When I walked away from my first business all those years ago, what I'd have loved would have been for someone to come alongside of me as I rebuilt my business. To support me. To guide me. To challenge me. To hold me accountable. To be there when I needed an ear to listen, a shoulder to cry on, an arm to hug me. To happy dance and celebrate with me.

Whether you're looking to start over, whenever you're navigating change, the truth is you can't do it alone. The truth bomb here is that if you could do it alone, you already would have.

Whatever you're wanting to change or improve in your life will be more effective, successful and bring you greater results when you have support in the process.

Without support, environment always wins. What that means is that when you're trying to do something, anything differently, situations arise that make it harder than you thought it would be. And when that happens, as it always does, if you don't have sufficient support, you'll quickly revert to doing it the way you always have because that's easier and it's just how we humans function.

> *"Community – the human connection – is the key to personal and career success."*
>
> *Paul J Meyer*

Community is a group of people having characteristics or interests in common.

Connection is relationship and/or bond attachment to a person, place, thing or belief. It can be deep and significant or loose and insignificant. The more closely connected I feel, the more meaningful it is to me.

Community of connection involves trust, reciprocity, collaboration, cooperation and familial support.

> *"Kind hearts are the gardens, kind thoughts are the roots, kind words are the blossoms, kind deeds are the fruits."*

Henry Wadsworth Longfellow

Our commitment and level of participation influences how significant this is for us, both in how much we give and what we allow ourselves to receive through our creativity with others in the community.

Community of connection is kind of like a figure of 8 that is interloped and tied together.

> "*Never believe that a few caring people can't change the world. For, indeed, that's all who ever have.*"
>
> *Margaret Mead*

Lone Wolf or Pack Animal?

A lone wolf is an animal or person who lives alone rather than with others in a pack.

The danger is that when you choose to be a lone wolf no one has your back!

> "*Relationships are the fertile soil from which all advancement, all success, all achievement in real life grows.*"
>
> *Ben Stein*

It takes a village to raise a child. We've heard that forever. We know it's true. Yet, we presume that we can raise our dream alone.

STOP TRYING TO DO IT ALL ALONE! You can't do it all alone! You just can't. Period.

I know you've probably tried for a long time to do it all alone. Maybe you thought you had to.

Maybe you didn't know anyone who understood you or your situation, or who was able, or wanted, to help and support you.

Believe me when I say I know how it feels. I know the loneliness of doing it all alone. I know the busyness of work. On the outside, my businesses appeared successful, but I sure didn't feel successful on the inside.

I was running around like a headless chook, trying to be all things to all people. Keeping everyone happy. Customers. Staff. Family. Children. Suppliers. Everyone but me!

I felt stuck where I was and I didn't know how to get unstuck! You see, I'd gone as far as I could alone. Hey, I'd even looked for help. But I couldn't find the kind of help I knew I needed to get me where I wanted to be.

That's why I do what I do. Now I serve and support women, in ways I'd have loved all those years ago.

> "*Every successful individual knows that his or her achievement depends on a community of persons working together.*"
>
> *Paul Ryan*

I understand how unhelpful and unsupportive the blank looks, often accompanied by nodding, are when you tell those close to you what it's like for you. They just don't get it; they can't get it. Their experience of life is not the same as yours. Their intention is good. They listen and try to understand to the best of their ability; yet because they haven't experienced it for themselves, they just can't get it. It's not their fault. It's not yours. It just is!

There are times in life when all the friends and family in the world, providing all the love and support they can, is just not enough. Truth is, there are moments, periods of time, when friends and family can't provide support for you in the most appropriate way.

Sometimes you need support of a different kind. Of all the things successful people do to accelerate their success and create their dream life, working with a coach is at the top of their list. Coaching is well known in the sports arena and yet, not so well known in the personal and business arena. Be assured that coaching will help you get from where you are to where you want to be, faster and easier. A coach will help you discover what you truly want and help you identify the steps and actions required to get there.

> "I absolutely believe that people, unless coached, never reach their maximum capabilities."
>
> Bob Nardelli

When you do find the best support for you, you'll know, and you'll cherish it as it in turn sustains, nourishes and strengthens you.

Just as he was thinking what a beautiful day it was, a red flag poked up from the grass and waved hard.

Tootle stopped, for every locomotive knows he must Stop for a Red Flag Waving.

"I'll go another way," said Tootle.

He turned to the left, and up came another waving red flag, this time from the middle of the buttercups.

When he went to the right, there was another red flag waving.

There were red flags waving from the buttercups, in the daisies, under the trees, near the bluebirds' nest, and even one behind the rain barrel.

And of course, Tootle had to stop for each one, for a locomotive must always Stop for a Red Flag Waving.

"Red flags," muttered Tootle. "This meadow is full of red flags. How can I have any fun? Whenever I start, I have to stop. Why did I think this meadow was such a fine place? Why don't I ever see a green flag?"

Just as the tears were ready to slide out of his boiler, Tootle happened to look back over his coal car. On the tracks stood Bill, and in his hand was a big green flag.

"Oh!" said Tootle. He puffed up to Bill and stopped.

"This is the place for me," said Tootle. "There is nothing but red flags for locomotives that get off their tracks."

Bill had Tootle's back. He was looking out for him. Supporting him. Who's 'got your back'? Who helps you keep going when the going gets tough?

In my experience, both in my life and my clients' lives, the going gets tough always when you least expect it. Or you're less able to cope with it. Often, that's because there's lots of other challenges going on in your life at the same time.

Who will help you then? As a result of my experiences, I went on a quest, an adventure, discovering what would have helped me then. My mission now is to share what I discovered with women so they don't have to go through anything like I went through.

Now Tootle is a famous Two-Miles-a-Minute Flyer. The young locomotives listen to his advice.

"Work hard," he tells them. "Always remember to Stop for a Red Flag Waving. But most of all, Stay on the Rails No Matter What."

As Bill had supported Tootle, so Tootle was now able to support the young locomotives in training. When Tootle was spending his days playing in the meadow, he was not aligned with his vision of becoming a famous Flyer.

Without support, we too can get off the rails and although we can appear busy and successful, that is not always our reality.

With Bill's support, and the support of every person living in the village of Lower Trainswitch, Tootle got back on the rails so that he could realize his vision and achieve his goal.

Truth is, you won't be able to do it alone, any more than Tootle could. Truth is, you'll go backwards if you try to do it all alone.

Without Bill and everyone else supporting him, without

community and connection, Tootle may never have become the famous Flyer that he dreamed of being.

Even when you do make progress alone, it will be less speedy or less substantial, or both, than you would make if you had help, support and accountability. If someone else has your back; someone who's not involved with you in any other way, then they're able to be fully objective and focused on your best interests. While that won't always mean finding the easy way out, it will mean supporting you through the route that will most benefit you and your business.

When you don't have adequate, appropriate support, you struggle along alone. You try to encourage yourself to keep going when the going gets tough. You use lots of tips and tricks to keep yourself accountable for taking action. You will make progress as long as you continue implementing and taking action. However, you will not gain the traction or growth you dream of. Inevitably, you'll arrive at a destination, although it may not be the success you dream of.

> "Instead of drifting along like a leaf in a river, understand who you are and how you come across to people and what kind of an impact you have on the people around you and the community around you and the world, so that when you go out, you can feel you have made a positive difference."
>
> Jane Fonda

Here's what I know to be true. Those of us who have a coach keep on going. Those of us who are part of mastermind groups keep on going. We make progress faster, smoother and easier than when we try to do it alone.

We keep taking action. We know they've got our backs. We know they're going to quiz us and question us about what we've done and what we haven't done. We don't want to disappoint our coach or our fellow masterminders, and so we do what otherwise would probably not get done in the same time frame.

> "When two or more people coordinate in a spirit of harmony and work toward a definite objective or purpose, they place themselves in position, through the alliance, to absorb power directly from the great storehouse of infinite intelligence."
>
> Napoleon Hill

A mastermind is a small, intimate group of people who meet regularly for the purpose of problem solving, brainstorming, networking, encouraging and motivating each other. Masterminding is one of the most powerful tools for successfully creating your dream life.

There's tremendous power in having a coach and belonging to a mastermind. Having a coach is an investment that will repay you many times over what you invest to retain your coach. As will being part of a mastermind group.

> "It takes collaboration in a community to develop better skills for better lives."
>
> Jose Angel Gurria

Connections can be deep and significant or loose and

insignificant. For most people, the more closely connected they feel, the more meaningful that connection is for them.

Our connections impact everything we do and how we understand the world around us whether we're aware of it or not.

When we're part of a community of connection, we're stronger, both as a group and as individuals.

> *"Live-tweeting your bikini wax is not vulnerability. Nor is posting a blow-by-blow of your divorce. That's an attempt to hot-wire connection. But you can't cheat real connection. It's built up slowly. It's about trust and time."*
>
> *Brene Brown*

Community and connection are essential for trust, collaboration, reciprocity, familial support and all sorts of other juicy benefits to exist and be received by members.

> *"The greatness of community is most accurately measured by the compassionate actions of its members."*
>
> *Coretta Scott King*

A community of connection, as I understand and implement it, is like the round table made famous in the Arthurian legend of King Arthur and his Knights of the Round Table. The table has no head because everyone who sits there has equal status. Everyone who was invited to sit at that table was regarded as trustworthy.

King Arthur and his Knights collaborated. They contributed to each other and to their common cause. They gave genuine familial support and love to one another. They trusted each other implicitly.

> *"In nature we never see anything isolated, but everything is in connection with something else which is before it, beside it, under it and over it."*
>
> *Johann Wolfgang von Goethe*

Chapter Summary

- Your connections impact everything you are and everything you do.
- Community support strengthens you.

Reflect

- What's the effect on you, of trying to do it all alone?
- Where would you benefit from support?
- What does an ideal community of connection include for you?

Implement

- Find and engage a coach.
- Find and join a mastermind group.

> *"I'm every woman. It takes a village to make me who I am."*
>
> *Katy Perry*

19. Continuing on your PATH

"Nothing in your past is in your present making you do anything you don't choose to do. You are not your past history! You are not your past failures! You are not how others have at one time treated you! You are only who you are and what you do now in this moment."

Karen Salmansohn

Changing the patterns and habits of a lifetime takes time. We're talking longer than the 21 to 90 days many claim it takes to form a new habit.

In the absence of support, our natural tendency is to revert back to our old patterns and behaviors. To slip back into our comfort zone.

"In the absence of support, environment always wins."

Jay Fiset

Implementing new concepts into your life is challenging when you're living in an environment that hasn't changed. While you've changed through the course of reading and applying this book, your family and friends haven't changed.

Who will you turn to for support when your partner, family, friends or team aren't supportive?

What will you do when other people expect you to behave in ways you always have, and you no longer do?

How will you respond when the itty-bitty-shitty committee in your head refuses to be quiet?

How will you quiet the shoulda, coulda, woulda voice when it niggles at you?

Trying to do it alone makes it harder than it needs to be. Doing it on your own is difficult, lonely and not at all enjoyable. You're most probably like me and know that from past experience.

Choosing your own path means choosing to be different from your past self and to do things differently.

Committing to creating your own path and living your life on your terms is an ongoing process. Making this a pleasurable process in your life is almost guaranteed when you have ongoing support from an exclusive, intimate group of courageous and brilliant, daring and resilient, like-hearted women who are devoted to living their dream and making great money in the process.

A *creatress* is a woman or goddess who creates, produces or constitutes something.

A courageous creatress is a woman who lives her life in accordance with her own values and beliefs.

A profitable creatress is a woman who makes great money doing work she loves and who loves her life.

Procrastination is the enemy of decision. When you procrastinate, you're choosing not to decide. When you choose not to decide you've chosen for things to remain the same.

My encouragement is for you to keep on being courageous as you blossom into who you truly are and refuse to hide the treasure you are, as you share your unique gifts and offerings with the world, living life on your terms and following your own path.

Choose and decide – there is no other way.

Afterword

A final word from Daphne, your *Inspiritress of Can-do-it-ness.*

Throughout this book you've read stories of women who've successfully created lives they love on their own terms, through using the PATH approach. None of them have done this on their own; they've asked for and received support, either personally from me or through one of my programs.

Even though you're now at an advantage by having learned the PATH approach through reading this book, choosing to do it alone means it will be harder than it needs to be.

I'd love to invite you to join me and your fellow courageous creatresses in the VIP room at https://daphnewells.com where you'll receive gifts, big discounts, inspiring emails and exclusive surprises, available only for my VIPs.

To support courageous creatresses to choose your own path, I've created a program where you'll receive the support you need while you form new habits, and implement what you've learned through reading this book. This is for courageous and ambitious women, like you, who are ready to step up and lead your own life. You're serious and excited about creating a life you love, doing work you love and making great money in the process, whilst also having a heap of fun; and you're an action taker, a decision maker and a go-getter.

For more information and other ways to receive help and

support from me, including book bonuses, visit https://daphnewells.com

You can do this!

I believe in you xx

Daphne

About Daphne Wells

Daphne, your *Inspiritress of Can-do-it-ness*, is a certified professional coach, facilitator and mastermind leader with a history of birthing and growing small businesses. She has a deep passion to empower eminent leaders.

Her true magic lies in her ability to clarify, to see possibilities, to create ideas and to inspirit you to implement. She sees the best in you and believes in you, no matter what.

Some years ago, Daphne quietly and effectively changed an industry; opening doors for women in a previously male-dominated field. Now, she guides leaders to be more effective in their roles.

Courageous and ambitious women business owners, leaders, coaches, service professionals, therapists and entrepreneurs around the globe, all of whom have big hearts and yearn to make a difference and to make money, hire Daphne so they can successfully start over or pivot for growth without sacrificing themselves in the process.

Daphne lives near the beach in the beautiful South Island of New Zealand, from where she serves and supports women worldwide.

www.daphnewells.com

www.linkedin.com/in/daphnewells

www.facebook.com/daphnebwells

www.instagram.com/daphnebwells

CPSIA information can be obtained
at www.ICGtesting.com
Printed in the USA
BVHW041924161219
566839BV00012B/170/P